CELTIC E
Saints & 1

Celtic Earth, Celtic Heaven

Saints & Heroes of the Powys Borderland

Patrick Thomas

First impression—2003

ISBN 1 84323 229 4

This book is published with the financial support of the Welsh Books Council.

Printed in Wales at
Gomer Press, Llandysul, Ceredigion SA44 4QL

Er cof am
JOHN BRYAN THOMAS
1919-88
a aned yng nghysgod Cefn Digoll

CONTENTS

INTRODUCTION

And the winds say, It is April, bringing scents
Of dead heroes and dead saints . . .
Despite our speech we are not English . . .
. . . on the cracked screen
Of life our shadows are large still
In history's fierce afterglow.

R. S. Thomas, 'Border Blues' from *Collected Poems* (J. M. Dent)

I was born in Welshpool and spent the first few years of my life in the village of Buttington, which is just on the Welsh side of the border with England. Coming from border country inevitably means that you are very much aware of your identity. Had I been born a few miles to the east, I would have been a 'Shropshire lad.' But I was born on the Welsh side of the border formed by the Long Mountain or Cefn Digoll ('The Unlost Hillside'). That meant that I was Welsh, even though the last Welsh-speaker in my family had been my great-grandfather.

At the age of seven I moved to England. Still the awareness of being Welsh persisted. For me, Wales was not the mountains of Gwynedd, the cliffs of Pembrokeshire or the valleys of the industrial South. My Wales was a little strip of eastern Montgomeryshire. It consisted of some fields by a river that would sometimes burst its banks and flood the surrounding area. It also included a market town where I first went to church and school and which had once seemed to be the bustling centre of the world.

I went to Cambridge to read English. My father was horrified. He asked me 'Why are you studying English when you can't even speak your own language?' The result was that I took a course in Medieval Welsh taught by the meticulous and brilliant Dr Rachel Bromwich. It deepened my fascination with Wales, its culture and history. A parallel spiritual journey led to my eventual ordination as a priest of the Church in Wales. One of the conditions of my acceptance as an ordinand was a commitment to become fluent in Welsh.

Some years ago I wrote a couple of studies of the spirituality of early Welsh Christianity, with a particular emphasis on west Wales. This new book was originally intended to focus on the traditions of the saints of the borderland of eastern Montgomeryshire: Gwyddfarch and Tysilio, Gwrnerth and Llywelyn and the early career of Beuno. But as I sifted the background material, I discovered, like R. S. Thomas before me, that in the borderland the 'scents of dead heroes and dead saints' are inextricably intermingled. For a thousand years, from the sixth to the sixteenth century, there was a constant tension there between heroism and holiness (as well as a great deal of savagery that was neither heroic nor holy).

So the book became a study of both the saints and the heroes of the borderland of what was once Powys Wenwynwyn. It is written to coincide with the visit of the National Eisteddfod to Meifod, and is intended for those border people who (like my father and grandfather) might wish to echo the poet's words: 'Despite our speech we are not English.' It is also meant for anyone else who wishes to catch a glimpse of the extraordinary spiritual, cultural and historical wealth of a beautiful, but often forgotten, area of Wales.

Writing about a part of the world that I left at the age of seven is a dangerous enterprise. I apologise for any inadvertent errors that may raise the blood pressure of dedicated local historians. Translating poetry (particularly Welsh poetry) is an equally hazardous task. The past few years have seen the publication of a remarkable number of scholarly editions of medieval Welsh poetry by the Canolfan Uwchefrydiau Cymreig a Cheltaidd in Aberystwyth.[1] In trying to produce modern English translations, I have leant heavily on the modern Welsh versions contained in many of these volumes. I owe an enormous debt of gratitude in particular to the work of Nerys Ann Jones, Ann Parry Owen, Gruffydd Aled Williams, A. Cynfael Lake, Rhiannon Ifans and R. Iestyn Daniel. Other literary scholars on whose work I have depended include Jenny Rowland, R. Geraint Gruffydd, Gwyn Thomas and the late Sir Ifor Williams.

My greatest debt of all is owed to Marged Haycock. She was the first person to undertake the thankless and apparently hopeless task of teaching me to speak modern Welsh over a quarter of a century ago. Her scholarship remains a source of wonder and inspiration, and it was through her anthology of early Welsh religious poetry that I was first introduced to Gwrnerth and Llywelyn and the seed of this book was sown. Any flaws, faults and infelicities in the translations are entirely my own. I have not attempted to replicate the metrical and verbal patterns that characterize so much of early Welsh verse but have aimed to give the sense of the poetry as directly as possible, whilst also respecting the line-by-line movement of the original. Inevitably, much of its beauty will have been lost in the process. I am especially grateful to Jane Cartwright for reading the typescript and making a great many valuable and helpful suggestions and corrections, and also to Ceri Wyn Jones of Gwasg Gomer for his friendly assistance, guidance, wisdom and patience. I would also like to express my appreciation of the kind and courteous help provided by the staff of the National Library of Wales, Aberystwyth, Lampeter University Library and Carmarthen Public Library.

As a priest in a somewhat hectic urban parish, I am thankful for the assistance and encouragement of some of my colleagues in the ministry. Archbishop Rowan Williams rescued me from the depths of depression and suggested that I should start writing again. Bishop Carl Cooper also gave me his support, and the Very Reverend Wyn Evans, Dean of St Davids, generously allowed me to devote a stint as canon-in-residence to writing and research. My amazingly cheerful curate, the Reverend Ceri Davies, and my long-suffering parishioners in St David's and Christ Church, Carmarthen, are also deserving of a great deal of gratitude. My wife Helen and our children Iori, Gareth, Llinos, Mair and Gwenllian, have valiantly put up with the abstraction and absent-mindedness of a husband and father whose thoughts were often far away in the mists of medieval Powys when they should have been closer to home.

This book is dedicated to the memory of my own father, John Bryan Thomas. He was born in Garth Derwen, at the foot of the Long Mountain, and had a deep awareness and appreciation of the history of the eastern Montgomeryshire borderland. Our first family home was Maes Hafren, a house that he had built on the field that is the setting for *Breuddwyd Rhonabwy*. My father was not very happy when I became a priest, but he forgave me because I returned to Wales and learned the language that he himself had never quite managed to master. Like many fathers and sons, we were not always good at communicating with one another. Nevertheless I hope that he would have approved of the pages that follow.

NOTES

[1] The volumes contained in *Cyfres Beirdd y Tywysogion* and *Cyfres Beirdd yr Uchelwyr*.

1. GWYDDFARCH AND TYSILIO

i) The Two Gwyddfarchs

In 1536 John ap Rhys, a Cistercian abbot, set out from Ystrad Marchell (Strata Marcella) on the banks of the Severn near Welshpool to ride to London. His task was a painful one. He was being forced to surrender his monastery and its lands to a king and government hungry for church property. The religious community founded by Owain Cyfeiliog in 1170 was to be dissolved.[1] Before long only a few piles of rubble would remain to mark the place where monks had prayed for so many centuries. The famous image of Christ that once had drawn pilgrims from both sides of the Welsh border to Ystrad Marchell would vanish forever.

Abbot John must have recalled a very different journey to London that he had made in 1528. At that time he had been in charge of the monastery for three years. The young, devout and scholarly man had been shocked by the condition of Ystrad Marchell when he arrived there. Many of the buildings were in ruins and the three remaining monks lived in the echoing shell of a past glory. John ap Rhys had decided to take decisive action to rescue his new home.

The most effective way to raise money for a religious cause at that time was by persuading the Pope to issue an indulgence. This would guarantee spiritual privileges of various kinds to anyone who fulfilled its conditions. An intense religious storm had already broken out on the Continent after Martin Luther's attack on the theological validity of combining fund-raising with an offer of salvation. Luther's radical ideas had already reached Cambridge. There the young theologian Robert Barnes had enthusiastically adopted them and had been imprisoned as a result.[2] But they had not yet penetrated as far as the decaying monastery just over the Welsh border.

The abbot had had no problem in obtaining the issue of an indulgence for all those who visited Ystrad Marchell as pilgrims or who gave the community practical or financial help and support. He merely asked his father, Robert ap Rhys, to have a word with his close friend Cardinal Wolsey, who was still the most powerful prelate in the land. Wolsey then squared matters with Pope Clement VII and the indulgence was granted.

John's father, Robert ap Rhys, was one of the most influential Welsh ecclesiastics of the time. He was both vicar-general of St Asaph diocese and Cardinal Wolsey's personal chaplain. In theory of course priests were supposed to be celibate. Robert ap Rhys (like many other Welsh clergy of the time) quietly ignored this regulation. He fathered a large family. Three of his sons became noted members of the Welsh squirearchy and two others became Cistercian abbots in Wales while their father was still alive. No one in authority seems to have batted an eyelid at this. Robert retained his important position in the Welsh church and beyond.[3]

His son was not afraid of the new technology that was beginning to revolutionise the spread of ideas and information. Martin Luther had used the printing press to great effect in his attack on indulgences. John ap Rhys decided to use the same instrument to promote his own particular indulgence and salvage his monastery from its desperate financial position. He rode to London and handed a copy to the printer Richard Pynson. The result was the first known printed document relating to Wales. Its contents are described by Sir Glanmor Williams as 'hazardously comprehensive' in their generosity to those who supported Ystrad Marchell.[4]

Eight years later things were very different. Wolsey's power had suddenly collapsed after he proved unable to obtain the Pope's support for Henry's divorce. The great Cardinal died in disgrace. Being his personal chaplain's son was no longer the key to influence in high places, indeed it was now something to keep very quiet about. The Henrician Reformation began and monastic property was one of its first targets. Ystrad Marchell was to be dissolved.

John ap Rhys was to receive compensation for the loss of his position as abbot. He would be appointed Dean of Pontesbury in Shropshire. It was a position that may well have been not quite as grand as its title implies. As he headed towards London, the abbot was aware that the demise of Ystrad Marchell had a far deeper significance than the transfer of property and the exchanging of ecclesiastical titles. The last of the documents relating to Ystrad Marchell reveals that John ap Rhys had another name. It is a lease in which he describes himself as 'John

Goyddvarche, abbot of Stratamarcella'.[5] 'Goyddvarche' was a Tudor scribe's version of the Welsh name Gwyddfarch. The original Gwyddfarch had lived in the late sixth and early seventh century and was the first recorded abbot in eastern Montgomeryshire. John ap Rhys, *alias* Gwyddfarch, was aware that he was part of a spiritual tradition in his area of Powys that stretched back for at least a thousand years and that now seemed finally to be coming to an end.

A few miles to the west of the site of Ystrad Marchell in the valley of the river Efyrnwy (Vyrnwy) is the village of Meifod. In the days when Powys was an independent principality, Meifod was its religious centre. Meifod was for Powys what Tyddewi (St Davids) was for Dyfed and Bangor was for Gwynedd: one of the great holy places of Wales. The most famous description of Meifod was written at the time when the ancient Celtic foundation was in danger of losing its spiritual supremacy to the new Cistercian monastery on the banks of the Severn. Cynddelw Brydydd Mawr (fl. 1155-95), of whom we shall hear a great deal more later, was characteristically extravagant in his praise:

> I love a church and its mighty clerics,
> By Gwyddfarch's holy place beyond Gwynedd:
> A princely wooded place, an honourable churchyard,
> A burying place for princes after the bravery of battle,
> The desire of poets, a place where many live,
> Where there are generous provisions, a place for the courageous,
> A privileged monastery on open ground with living space,
> Blessed Meifod, no cowardly men possess it!
>
> No violence rules it, no enemies can enter it,
> The dwelling place of the three saints will never pay such men homage,
> The hospitable welcome within is splendid patronage
> With no dishonourable intention:
> Its fine enclosure between its lovely streams,
> Its dignified and zealously devout inhabitants,
> Its gorgeous, much-privileged church,
> Its beautiful dignity and its immeasurably splendid gifts,
> Its lovely dawn after the depths of night,
> Its fine chancel a safe sanctuary from violence,
> Its dignified priests and their services
> And the loveliness of its Mass . . .[6]

The 'three saints' mentioned by Cynddelw were the three patrons of Meifod: Gwyddfarch, Tysilio and the Virgin Mary. Of these Gwyddfarch was regarded as having been responsible for turning Meifod into a religious centre. Folklore has ensured that his mark remains on the local landscape. Above the village is a hill where tradition has it that Gwyddfarch settled as a hermit. It is still known as Gallt yr Ancr ('The Hermit's Hill'). On the hill is a spot known as Gwely Gwyddfarch ('Gwyddfarch's Bed') where the holy man is said to have slept and eventually died.

Gwyddfarch's origins are unknown. In the medieval genealogies of the Welsh Saints, he is rather improbably described as the son of Amalrus, Prince of Apulia in Italy. In the seventeenth century, a hagiographer named Albert Le Grand wrote a life of St Suliau (Tysilio) based on readings used in the liturgies of two Breton dioceses. The picture that he paints of Meibot (Meifod) reflects the twelfth-century shrine and community described by Cynddelw rather than the place where Gwyddfarch and Tysilio lived in the sixth century. Albert describes it as a large town, saying that the princes of the area had endowed a rich abbey nearby. This was under the rule of Guymarchus (Gwyddfarch).[7]

A rather more plausible description of the situation in Gwyddfarch's time is given by the Venerable D. R. Thomas, archdeacon of Montgomery, historian of the Diocese of St Asaph and a Victorian vicar of Meifod. He records that there were three separate churches within the enclosure at Meifod. One was dedicated to Tysilio and another to the Virgin Mary. The third and earliest church was Eglwys Gwyddfarch. Thomas suggests that the building was originally 'the oratory of that ancient anchorite, a primitive structure of wattled reeds and clay, in which he gathered together his early converts for the service of prayer and praise, until it was superseded by the more substantial and imposing edifice which Tysilio built in the seventh century, and of which it then became a capella.' He quotes seventeenth-century documents which show that by the 1630s the ancient chapel had been turned into a house and that thirty years later the churchyard was being used as 'a hempe garden' by its neighbours.[8]

Gwyddfarch may originally have gone to Meifod looking for solitude. Jesus himself spent forty days in the wilderness at the beginning of his ministry and later he regularly escaped from the crowds to pray in silence on lonely hillsides. His example was remembered and recovered when St Anthony disappeared into the Egyptian desert deliberately turning his back on a corrupt and corrupting world and an increasingly corrupt church. Athanasius' biography of Anthony helped to spread this ideal across Europe. The lives and sayings of the Fathers and Mothers of the deserts of Egypt and Syria became part of the currency of Christian thought. In the west, Martin of Tours, the ex-soldier turned hermit and then reluctant bishop, became the pattern for ascetics. He too was the subject of a popular biography, written by Sulpicius Severus. Ascetic ideas reached Wales and Ireland from Gaul and perhaps from the Eastern Mediterranean as well. Hermits, living in solitude or in loosely knit communities, began to become a part of the Welsh religious landscape.

One of the best known of these hermits, who also lived in Powys, may possibly have been a contemporary of Gwyddfarch's. The cult of Melangell or Monacella is associated with Cwm Pennant, a remote valley several miles to the north west of Meifod. Her story has been preserved in carvings on the fifteenth-century rood screen in Pennant Melangell church and in a Latin life that has most recently been dated to the late fifteenth or early sixteenth century. Her shrine was restored in 1958 and again in 1991 from fragments that had been preserved when they were incorporated into the lych-gate and the walls of the church. It has been suggested that the shrine was originally built in the twelfth century by local craftsmen.[9]

Melangell's life may well have been composed in an attempt to preserve the status of her church as a place of sanctuary. Her legend has parallels in many other traditions about hermits and hunters from across Europe. It would appear to come from a long tradition of local storytelling in which it was used to explain who the saint was and why the valley in which she lived had special privileges and traditions linked to it. Readings containing incidents from Melangell's life were no doubt used in the liturgy at her shrine on the occasions when her festival was celebrated.

Her story is an attractive one. We are told that in the year 604 the prince of Powys was named Brochwel (or Brochfael) Ysgithrog. This date is problematic (the chronology of early Welsh history is often fraught with problems). The genealogical scholar Peter Bartrum has suggested the year 490 as the probable date of Brochwel's birth.[10] In that case, if Brochwel is more than a convenient peg for a storyteller to hang a legend on, the events described must have taken place some three-quarters of a century before 604. Brochwel's capital was Pengwern Powys, which the narrator informs us is now Shrewsbury.

One day the prince went hunting in Cwm Pennant, which was one of the most distant corners of his principality. His hunting dogs started a hare and chased it until it disappeared into a thorny bramble bush. Brochwel was probably rather surprised to see, in the midst of the brambles, a beautiful virgin absorbed in prayer and contemplation. The hare had taken refuge under the hem of the woman's garment. From that safe vantage point it looked out calmly and fearlessly at the dogs. The prince tried to urge his hounds on. They took no notice of his commands and instead retreated whimpering and howling. The carving on the rood screen suggests that Brochwel may have urged his huntsman to blow his horn to encourage the frightened dogs. The instrument apparently stuck to the unfortunate man's lips. This last addition to the original life also appears in the version of Melangell's story recorded by the eighteenth-century antiquary Thomas Pennant.[11]

All this came as a bit of a shock to the prince. He asked the woman how long she had lived on her own in such a desolate and remote part of his territory. She answered that she had been there for fifteen years and that she had not seen anyone else in all that time. Brochwel then asked who she was. She replied that she was the daughter of an Irish king who had wanted to marry her off to a rich nobleman. To avoid such a match she had run away, ending up in the valley where he had found her, and had dedicated herself to serving God and the Virgin Mary there.

Brochwel was impressed. He praised Melangell's truthfulness and Christian devotion. He regarded the way in which the hare had been preserved from his bloodthirsty hounds as a sign from God. The prince then gave her Cwm Pennant as a place of sanctuary for any man or woman who fled there seeking refuge, provided they did not violate or abuse their privilege. This element in the story probably reflects medieval concerns. Huw Pryce has shown that questions about ecclesiastical sanctuary were of particular concern to the compilers of lawbooks in early thirteenth-century Gwynedd.[12] Powys was a violent and troubled place during the same period. There may well have been quite a number of desperate asylum seekers who were only too glad to be able to find safety in a refuge that derived its authority from the Melangell legend.

The saint herself became known for her friendship with wild animals, particularly the hares that lived in her valley. Her reputed fondness for them left its mark on local folklore. A seventeenth-century writer noted that the local name for hares was 'Melangell's lambs'. The killing of hares was forbidden in the parish. If anyone came across someone hunting a hare with dogs they would shout out 'God and Saint Melangell be with thee,' and the hare would always escape.[13]

According to her hagiographer, Melangell gathered a community of like-minded women around her in Cwm Pennant. They lived a life of prayer and devotion presumably centred on the saint's cell, which after her death became her shrine and church. The spiritual geography of Pennant Melangell is not unlike that of Meifod. Just as Meifod has Gallt yr Ancr and Gwely Gwyddfarch so Cwm Pennant has Gwely Melangell on the hillside just below Craig Melangell ('Melangell's Rock') which overlooks the church. In both cases the Gwely and Gallt/Craig were natural features which were reputed to be places to which the hermit retreated for periods of solitude and prayer (or both). Holy men and women attract disciples, as the Egyptian Desert Fathers and Mothers had soon discovered. Melangell and Gwyddfarch were also portrayed as having become the focus of communities. In his old age Gwyddfarch was said to have acquired an unexpected disciple: Tysilio, son of the very Brochwel Ysgithrog whose hunting expedition in Cwm Pennant had had such an unexpected outcome.

ii) Tysilio: the Pacifist Prince and the Warrior Saint

A thousand years separate Tysilio and Albert Le Grand, his Breton biographer. Meifod is a long way from Brittany. A good story can survive for many centuries and travel a considerable distance. Inevitably it gets polished, embellished or altered in the process. Nevertheless Albert's hagiography does seem to contain elements of some rather unexpected ideas that may have been beginning to surface in Powys in Tysilio's time.[14]

Albert tells us that Suliau was the eldest of three brothers, and thus the one whom it was presumed would succeed Brocmail as prince of Powys. However Gwyddfarch, abbot of the local monastery, was a frequent visitor at the royal court. He and Tysilio used to discuss religious matters and the holy man's spiritual counsel had such an impact on the crown prince that he decided to join Gwyddfarch's community. The abbot was delighted when Tysilio told him of his decision. However a major problem remained. Tysilio knew that Brochwel would never permit him to become a monk. His only option was to trick his father. He pretended that he was going out hunting with his two brothers. When the three of them were a safe distance away from the court, Tysilio told the others what he was going to do. He then said goodbye to them and set off to the monastery.

When he arrived there, Tysilio asked Gwyddfarch to clothe him in the monastic habit immediately so that he could forestall any attempt by his father to force him to return to the royal court. The abbot agreed and the ceremony was performed without delay. Meanwhile Tysilio's brothers had reported back to Brochwel. The prince was furious. He despatched a war band of three hundred horsemen to recover his son from the monastery in Meifod. They had orders to decapitate Gwyddfarch if the abbot refused to co-operate or attempted any kind of resistance.

Gwyddfarch received this army with exemplary courtesy. He told them that Tysilio had come to the community of his own accord. Nevertheless he would summon him. If the young prince wished to hand back his monastic habit and return to the court with the soldiers, nothing would be done to hinder him. On the other hand if Tysilio wished to remain in Meifod, the abbot said that he would rather sacrifice his own life than try to make the young prince leave.

Tysilio duly appeared. He told Brochwel's henchmen that he was sorry that he had gone against his father's wishes. But then he reminded them of the Gospel injunction calling on people to leave their father and their mother for the sake of Christ. This, he said, made his action a pious rather than an ungrateful one. Then Tysilio offered his own head for them to cut off and take home with them to appease Brochwel's anger. By this time the horsemen had cooled down. They rode back to Brochwel to report to him that Tysilio would rather die than give up his monastic habit. Brochwel realised that his son was as stubborn as he was and gave in. Tysilio was still anxious that his father might come after him. He asked Gwyddfarch to send him away to a safe place. The refuge that the abbot found him was an island in the Menai Straits, now known as Ynys Tysilio, where the anxious monk found sanctuary for seven years.

At the other end of Wales where Pembrokeshire meets Carmarthenshire is a village named Llandysilio-yn-Nyfed. There is a tradition that this is another place that Tysilio visited while hiding from Brochwel. This led Waldo Williams, one of the greatest twentieth-century Welsh poets, to compose a poem describing the fugitive's visit:

> Frequently I'm surprised. What light from beyond
>> Explained Christ to his elect
> When our lives were greedy and filthy
>> And our clay scarcely stamped with his thought or ideals.
> I remember how we'd go to the front door
>> When the church bell rang for a better year;
> Montgomeryshire's gentleness was on dear Dyfed again
>> As imagination went on its far journeys
> In the depths of night. We'd see the little company,
>> Without a fort to camp in, yoking the world as one.
> And amongst them we'd see splendidly shining white,
>> Aflame with rejoicing in the Son of Man,
> Exiled Tysilio who in Meifod long ago desired no throne,
>> Lest he be forced to draw a sword.[15]

Waldo Williams was himself a deeply committed pacifist who was prosecuted for refusal to pay taxes that might have contributed towards Britain's involvement in the Korean War. It was natural that he should see Tysilio as a kindred spirit.

There are strands in the early literature of Powys that support the theory that there may have been a genuine questioning of traditional heroic ideals as war-weariness set in. The subject of one of the cycles of poems that were probably composed in the area in the ninth or tenth century is an old man named Llywarch Hen. His twenty-four sons are killed in battle against the English.[16] Llywarch is keen to send them to fight, but after their deaths he sings a self-pitying song about his resulting loneliness. The general scholarly consensus is that the poems were once embedded in a prose saga that has since been lost.

One of the most interesting of the Llywarch poems is the debate between the old man and Gwên, his youngest and last surviving son. Gwên is far from keen to go to battle and Llywarch accuses him of deliberately wasting time in order to delay his departure. Gwên agrees to go and fight. His last remark, however, is a sideswipe at his old father, who is full of heroic talk and yet, unlike his sons, has somehow survived unscathed to a ripe old age. Gwên goes to fight at Rhyd Forlas and is duly killed like all the others, and Llywarch sings a lament in his honour. Sir Ifor Williams, one of the greatest interpreters of early Welsh poetry, hazarded a guess which he admitted was 'pure conjecture' that Gwên might have originally left home for a time to avoid the war. He cited the tradition about Tysilio as a parallel.[17]

There is a poem that appears in the thirteenth-century *Llyfr Du Caerfyrddin* ('Black Book of Carmarthen') which seems to have a place in the Llywarch Hen saga material. It has been the subject of considerable scholarly discussion. The verses talk about snow falling and covering a valley. The poem apparently contains a debate between Llywarch's son Mechydd and a guide named Pelis about the wisdom of fighting in such bitter winter weather. Warriors are setting off for battle. A voice (presumably Mechydd) remarks 'I do not go – a wound prevents me.' To which a second angry voice retorts that the shirker is neither a cleric nor an aged nobleman, sneering 'A pity, Cynddilig, that you were not a woman.'[18] Both Professor Kenneth Jackson and Dr Jenny Rowland suggest that the Cynddilig stanza has been interpolated and that it originally came from a poem in which Llywarch taunted another of his sons. It does indeed sound like the authentic voice of the bloodthirsty retired warrior. The reference to Cynddilig not being a cleric also seems to tie in with the Tysilio tradition. It reminds us of Tysilio's desperate request to be clothed immediately in a monastic habit before Brochwel's henchmen could get their hands on him and force him to return to court.

The verses about the two reluctant warriors inspired another twentieth-century Welsh pacifist poet, Thomas Gwynn Jones. In the mid-1930s, with the memory of the carnage of the First World War still fresh in people's minds, and the threat of a new war looming ever closer, he composed a poem entitled 'Cynddilig'.[19] In it the man who did not want to go into battle is portrayed as the twenty-sixth son of Llywarch Hen. Much to his father's disgust he has become a monk at Meifod. After the battle he goes to Rhyd Forlas and finds the bodies of Gwên and the Mercian warrior who had killed him and been killed by him.

> And in his anguish Cynddilig remembered
> the day his father spoke
> that word, in his pain and his old age,

in his anger when he was troubled
that in his last years had been born to him
a son who knew nothing of swordcraft,
but lingered in the monastic enclosure
in devotion and prayer,
while his brothers were all in the red battle,
sons of their father in his strength and hope,
his bravery in the days of his courage,
sons who would die if need compelled it . . .
'A pity, Cynddilig, that you were not a woman.'[20]

For a moment an instinctive primeval desire to exact revenge for his dead brother overwhelms the young monk. He pulls the bloodstained dagger from the heart of his brother's enemy and then plunges it back into the corpse's heart again with an exultant shout. And then he notices the blood on his hand and is filled with shame and horror. His father's words continue to haunt him:

Merciless words,
reproaching him with drawn-out mockery
for his futile ritual
and his vow taken in those days
of meditation and peace in Meifod,
with its wise learning and wonderful duties,
and the calm minds of its brothers . . .
'A pity, Cynddilig, that you were not a woman.'[21]

In his misery he remembers his childhood. The poet locates this in the part of Powys whose conquest and destruction by the Mercians is described in the Heledd saga (the subject of our next chapter). The religious centre of this area had been Eglwysau Basa (now the village of Baschurch in Shropshire):

he heard the bells of Eglwysau Basa
the song of the Brothers in the choir,
the shouts of the children as they played,
and the hounds barking in the woods.

And he saw Gwên between the trees,
with his small fair head,
and two blue eyes,
innocent, gentle, young,

with childhood's lovely chattering and laughter on his lips –
great God! Why were things not like that any more.

Gwên with his tame white doves,
coming to his hand,
or landing on his arm and his two shoulders,
talking and gently caressing his face
with their silken heads,
each one would answer to her name –
sisters playing with their brother –
Gwên! there was no wild thing
that would not be tame where Gwên was![22]

But both Gwên and his opponent are dead:

And what the two of them were has now escaped,
escaped from the passions of earth,
from the flaw of the incomplete will,
from the disunity of the divided self,
from the gnawing fear in the atoms of their substance,
from the passion that is in the world . . . [23]

As Cynddilig watches over the two bodies a flock of silent birds seems to
gather in the red moonlight above the battlefield.

And up from the cold corpses came,
as it were, two fair doves,
and ascended as if into the mystic retinue
of a civilised people.[24]

Cynddilig buries the two men and builds a cairn over them from ancient
stones that had once marked the graves of previous heroes: 'unknown
sacrifices to the rule of Fear.'

Powys is left silent and in mourning after this final defeat. Llywarch,
desolated by Gwên's death is 'old, sleepless, ill, bereft.' When Cynddilig
comes to look for him his father repeats the old insult:

'Cynddilig? A pity that in the day of grief,
he alone is left to me
of all my sons: and I, who once knew how
to bravely bear a spear –
am overcome by illness and old age,

a pity that I'm not forgotten in the grave,
and Cynddilig too . . . pity he wasn't a woman!'[25]

His last remaining son explains to Llywarch that he had come looking
for him to make sure that he was still alive. Suddenly there is a scream. A
female slave, her dress stained with her own blood, staggers into the hill-
fort where the old man has been sheltering. She kneels at Llywarch's feet
and begs for help. Then her pursuers arrive: an armed band of cruel
Mercians. Cynddilig goes forward and stands between the woman and
the warriors:

The monk raised his hand and quietly asked
'Do you see it as an achievement to hunt down slaves
and force yourselves on the unarmed?
Will this be your custom and your history?'[26]

The Mercians are struck dumb by the challenge of this unarmed man.
They can't make out whether he is a hero or a fool. Cynddilig turns
towards the slave and binds up her wounded arm. The Mercians begin to
feel ashamed and start to melt away. Only one stands his ground. He fires
an arrow that pierces Cynddilig's heart. The monk dies in his father's
arms. In his final lament Llywarch reveals that the rescued woman was a
Mercian slave of his. He changes his verdict on the son who had
sacrificed his life for her:

'A pity, Cynddilig, that you were not a leader
called in the day of need,
you who possessed
neither weapon
nor fear!'[27]

The poem ends with three white doves flying far above the earth.

T. Gwynn Jones's 'Cynddilig' is one of the most powerful poetic
expressions of Welsh pacifism in the twentieth century. It is based on the
contrast between monk and warrior: the heroism of the non-violent
man who is prepared to sacrifice himself as a matter of principle and the
heroism of the violent man who goes to war because patriotic necessity
demands it. The author's sympathy is clearly with the former. The poet
portrays Cynddilig as a monk of Meifod because Meifod is the
monastery of Tysilio, the prince who famously set his crown aside to

follow the peaceful way of Christ. Yet there is also evidence of a very different view of Tysilio in earlier times.

We have already come across Cynddelw's description of Meifod. It comes from *'Canu Tysilio'* – a poem sung in honour of Tysilio. Its most recent editors, Nerys Ann Jones and Ann Parry Owen, suggest that the poem was commissioned by the monastery at Meifod. The members of the community there were worried that their position as the religious centre of Powys was under threat. Previous rulers had always accepted the primacy of Tysilio's ancient foundation, but Owain Cyfeiliog was about to found and endow a rival community of the newly fashionable Cistercians at Ystrad Marchell. To defend their position, the monks of Meifod had to remind their ruler that Tysilio Sant was the true patron and protector of Powys. Cynddelw's poem had to emphasise this fact.

It did. Cynddelw stresses the peacefulness of Meifod itself. However he also portrays Tysilio as the saint whose protection helped the men of Powys to win the battle of Cogwy. Both Madog ap Maredudd of Powys and his son, Owain Cyfeiliog, were interested in the heroic age and the young Owain had a rather gung-ho approach to both warfare and poetry (as we shall see later). Depicting Tysilio as a patron of Powys's warriors was a way to kindle their interest and hopefully earn their support.[28]

However this Tysilio of battles may be nothing more than the product of twelfth-century political and ecclesiastical expediency. The Llywarch Hen poems come from an earlier period and suggest, at the very least, a rather ambiguous attitude towards traditional heroic values. The old man who sends his sons off to their death, taunting them where necessary to ensure their departure, is a distinctly unattractive figure. Perhaps Albert Le Grand's story (despite its late date) does indeed contain a memory of this critical questioning of long established heroic assumptions. The historic Tysilio is beyond recovery, but the possibility that he was an early Welsh Christian man of peace continues to strike a chord in the Welsh imagination.

iii) Gwyddfarch and Tysilio: Seeing the Holy City

Albert Le Grand tells us that, after Tysilio had been hiding away for seven years on his island in the Menai Straits, Gwyddfarch summoned his disciple back to Meifod. The old abbot wanted the younger man to take over the monastery while he went on a pilgrimage to Rome, for he had a deep desire to see the holy city before he died. There was nothing unusual about Gwyddfarch's proposed journey. The opening pages of the Welsh chronicle, *Brut y Tywysogyon*, are dotted with references to Welsh rulers visiting Rome. In the very first entry (dated 681-2) Cadwaladr the Blessed, son of Cadwallon ap Cadfan and last king of the Britons, is noted as having died in Rome. Cyngen, king of Powys, suffered the same fate there in 856, as did a certain Hywel thirty years later. The famous lawmaker Hywel Dda (920s) and Dwnwallon, king of Strathclyde (975), were more fortunate. They both visited Rome and apparently returned safe and sound.[29]

A poem from *Llyfr Du Caerfyrddin* gives a vivid and amusing picture of a somewhat neurotic and superstitious penitential Welsh pilgrim preparing to set out to Rome at a rather later date:

> The first phrase I say
> In the morning as I get up:
> 'May Christ's Cross be my armour.'
>
> Under God's protection I arm myself today.
> I feel a sneeze coming:
> It's not my God; I don't believe it.
>
> I arm myself splendidly.
> I don't believe in superstition – it's wrong to do so.
> The God who made me will give me strength.
>
> I have a mind to travel,
> I intend to cross the sea:
> A good intention: there'll be a prize there.
>
> My mind is perplexed,
> I intend to cross the sea:
> A good intention. He will be Lord.
>
> The crow lifts his wing,
> Intending to go far:
> A good intention. It will be better.
>
> The crow lifts its wing,
> Intending to go to Rome:
> A good intention: it will be lovely.

Saddle the bay stallion with white nostrils,
Eager to run and tough haired.
Lord of Heaven, we must have God with us.

Saddle the short-haired bay stallion,
Easy to handle amidst excitement, prancing along.
Where there's a nose there will be sneezing.

Saddle the long-jumping bay stallion,
Easy to handle in excitement, with an eager pace.
One unfortunate sneeze won't affect a brave man.

Earth's company is sad; the brier leaves are thick,
The sweet mead is a bitter draught from the drinking horn,
Lord of Heaven, make my journey easy!

O descendant of the Lord and winner of victory in battle,
And St Peter, chieftain of every nation,
And St Bride, bless my journey.

Son of intercession, Lord of my will,
Christ of Heaven, column and gift:
May my deed recompense for sin.[30]

The pilgrim was clearly extremely worried about the possible dangers of his journey.

When Tysilio returned to Meifod, he had grave doubts about Gwyddfarch's pilgrimage, fuelled by more substantial concerns than a possibly ill-omened sneeze or an assessment of the direction in which the crows were flying. The abbot was now an old man and the entries in the *Brut* would seem to indicate that the mortality rate among Welsh pilgrims to Rome was quite high. Tysilio was also anxious about what would happen to the monastery during Gwyddfarch's absence. He felt that without the holy man's wisdom and guidance the monks would be like poor and helpless orphans. He went to the abbot and made a suggestion. Would Gwyddfarch be satisfied if Tysilio somehow enabled him to see Rome, with all its beautiful churches and sumptuous palaces, without leaving Meifod? By now the abbot was aware that his disciple and friend strongly disapproved of the proposed journey. He therefore agreed to accept Tysilio's proposal.[31]

The younger monk spent the night in prayer in the monastery church asking God to grant Gwyddfarch a vision of Rome. On the following day Gwyddfarch joined Tysilio for a walk around the monastic enclosure. They came to a little hill within the enclosure and climbed it. It may be that the old man was feeling tired and fell asleep and dreamed what followed (as Baring-Gould and Fisher suggest), though the Breton hagiographer makes no reference to this.[32] He suggests that the two men shared the vision of the holy city. They both, he says, spent two hours on the hill, contemplating the wonders of Rome. They saw its great churches and palaces, its amphitheatres and obelisks and all the other rare and marvellous treasures that it possessed. Then the bell of the monastic church began to ring, summoning them out of their vision and back to the daily routine of Meifod. They made their way back down the hill and into the church for vespers.

Having had this vision, Gwyddfarch was quite content. His desire to see Rome was satisfied. He thanked Tysilio and God for the special favour that had been shown him. On the face of it the experience seems very strange indeed. It is perhaps not surprising that Baring-Gould and Fisher attempted to rationalise it into the wish-fulfilling dream of a tired old man. But Albert Le Grand's version is supported by some lines in Cynddelw's poem about Tysilio, which describes the vision as Gwyddfarch's disciple and companion saw it:

My eager adventurous man saw a beautiful sight,
What he saw will not be seen till the Day of Judgement,
The City of Rome, a wonderful sight,
A sublime fortress, with the most splendid ceremonies,
A spacious fortress, with bold inhabitants,
Its people do not follow sin,
A shining fortress, a strong unshakeable fortress,
A dwelling place praised from afar that is a fortress that shines from far away,
An honourable fortress where there is always a ready welcome,
A fortress made for pilgrimage.[33]

The shared vision of Gwyddfarch and Tysilio also contains elements that occur in other Welsh stories. The hillock for example is an obvious place from which to see visions and wonders. In the first branch of the *Mabinogion*, Pwyll Prince of Dyfed and a great many of his followers gather together at the court of Arberth for a great feast. After the first sitting Pwyll gets up to get some fresh air and climbs to the top of a little hill called Gorsedd Arberth, just above the court. One of the courtiers then tells him that that the mound has a strange characteristic. Any lord who sits on it will not go from there without one of two experiences. Either he will be painfully wounded or he will see a wonder of some kind. Pwyll decides to take the risk in the hope of seeing a wonder. Sure enough Rhiannon then rides by on her amazing white horse.[34] The little hill up which Tysilio leads Gwyddfarch to see his vision of Rome would appear to have the same kind of mysterious property as the mound at Arberth.

The vision itself echoes the experience of one of the greatest mythical Welsh figures. In 1773 Rhys Jones of Tyddyn Mawr, Llanfachreth, Meirionnydd, published an anthology of classical Welsh poetry taken from manuscripts that he had collected or copied. The handsome volume was entitled *Gorchestion Beirdd Cymru neu Flodau Godidowgrwydd Awen* ('The Feats of the Poets of Wales or Flowers of the Excellence of the Muse'). One of the subscribers to the book was none other than the English literary giant Doctor Samuel Johnson. Many of the others were scholarly Welsh-speaking clergy. Among the poems that Rhys Jones included was one called *Hanes Taliesin* ('The Story of Taliesin'). It begins:

> I am Elphin's chief public poet;
> My native land is the land of the cherubim;
> Johannes the wizard called me Myrddin;
> Now every king calls me Taliesin.
>
> I was with my Lord in the heights of heaven,
> When Lucifer fell to the depths of hell;
> I know the stars from the North to Auster;
> I was in a way before Alexander.
>
> I was in Gwydion's Fortress, Tetragramaton;
> I brought Heon down the Vale of Hebron;
> I was in Llydon before Gwydion was born:
> I was in Canaan when Absalom was killed.
>
> I was with my Lord in the ass's manger;
> I gave Moses power through the waters of Jordan;
> I said prayers for Eli and Enoch;
> I was on the cross of judgement, the son of merciful God.

I was the chief guardian at the battle of the Emerald Tower,
I spent three seasons in Arianrhod's Fortress:
I was in Gwynfryn, in Cynfelyn's Court;
I was the Harp Poet for Lleon of Llychlyn.

I bore hunger for the Son of the Virgin;
I was in Africa when Rome was built;
I came here to the ruins of Troy;
I was in the sky with Mary Magdalene.

I received the Muse from Ceridwen's Cauldron:
I was almost nine months in the witch Ceridwen's belly;
I used to be Gwion Bach, now I am Taliesin;
I was in the Ark with Noah and Alpha.

I saw Sodom and Gomorrah destroyed;
I saw the Trinity with my eyes;
I shall be on the face of the earth till the Day of Judgement,
It's not known if my flesh is meat or fish.[35]

Rhys Jones suggests that the author of this extraordinary poem was a poet named Taliesin, 'a man from the Parish of Rhychwyn, in Caernarfonshire, who flourished around 540 A.D.'[36]

There was a historical Taliesin who lived towards the end of the sixth century but he didn't come from Rhychwyn and he didn't have anything to do with the verses that appear above. Sir Ifor Williams identified a group of poems in the fourteenth-century manuscript known as *Llyfr Taliesin* ('The Book of Taliesin') which were written by this poet. Williams suggested that the historical Taliesin was probably a native of a Powys which stretched far beyond the present border between Wales and England and included Shropshire, Cheshire and possibly even South Lancashire. He seems to have begun his career as the court poet of Cynan Garwyn, prince of Powys.[37]

Cynan was the son of Brochwel Ysgithrog and grandson of Cyngen, and was therefore Tysilio's brother. He appears to have spent most of his time fighting his fellow Welshmen/Britons in South Wales, Anglesey and Cornwall instead of addressing the Saxon threat. Taliesin's poem is fascinating as a contemporary portrait of one of the sixth-century Cadelling, those members of the dynasty reputedly founded in the fifth century by Cadell Ddyrnllug, who was said to have been converted, baptised and blessed as a father of kings by St Garmon or Germanus.[38]

Cynan, protector in battle gave me a gift.
There is no lie in the great praise of the giver of homesteads,
a hundred fast stallions with silver saddles,
a hundred purple cloaks, each one the same size,
a hundred bracelets in my lap, fifty expensive ornaments,
a sword with a stone sheath, yellow-hilted, better than any:
all were had from Cynan: enemies hate to see him.
Men of Cadell's lineage, a steadfast army,
go to fight on the Wye with innumerable spears;
they strike the men of Gwent with blood-soaked blades.
A battle in great, fair Anglesey, famously praised;
so easy to take it having crossed the Menai.
A battle in Crug Dyfed King Aergol is shaken:
never before have his cattle been stolen.
Brochwel's territory-extending son desires possessions.
Let him attack Cornwall: their fate will not be good.
He threatens them until they pray for mercy.
Cynan is my patron, king of every army.
With his broad-flamed torch he lights a great fire.
A battle in Brychan's land is like a molehill to him.
Wretched tyrants quake before Cynan,
a protection in battle like a leviathan,
the same as Cyngen support of a broad land.
I heard people talking, everyone saying:
everywhere under the sun has been captured by Cynan.[39]

From Cynan's court, Taliesin moved to that of Urien, the heroic ruler of Rheged, a northern kingdom which probably included North Lancashire, Cumbria, a swathe of North Yorkshire and may have extended into what is now Scotland. Urien was involved in valiant resistance against the invading Northumbrians from the 570s to the 590s. He was treacherously murdered by a fellow Welsh king named Morgant or Morgan, who was apparently jealous of Urien's military prowess.[40] Taliesin wrote poems in praise of Urien including a powerful description of his victory at the battle of Argoed Llwyfain.[41] He also wrote a lament on the death of Urien's son and successor Owain, who did not survive his father for very long.[42] Taliesin also visited other courts and leaders (much to Urien's disgust). Two poems survive which he wrote in praise of Gwallawg, the courageous and embattled Lord of Elmet (Elfed), an area around Leeds which was the last remaining Welsh/British outpost west of the Pennines.[43]

If the historical Taliesin was a native of Powys and a contemporary of Tysilio's, the legendary Taliesin also seems to have had his roots there. Sir Ifor Williams identified fifteen poems linked to this second Taliesin in the fourteenth-century manuscript. One of them actually refers to the poet as having sung before Tysilio's father Brochwel at his court in 'the meadows of the Severn' – probably his capital at Pengwern. This used at one time to be identified as Shrewsbury, though the archaeologists Roger White and Philip Barker are among those who now suggest that the true site of Pengwern may really be the Berth, an Iron Age fort near Baschurch in Shropshire.[44]

Marged Haycock has produced a masterly study of *Llyfr Taliesin*.[45] She shows that the memory of the Taliesin as a professional court poet survived throughout the Middle Ages. The fact that he lived in the sixth century 'on the historical horizon of the Welsh' may have played a part in helping to develop the myths that attached themselves to him. She suggests that the poems that are linked to Taliesin's mythical persona were probably composed between the eighth and the eleventh century. Marged Haycock lists five characteristics of the mythical Taliesin. He possesses encyclopaedic knowledge, particularly of the exotic, the strange and the obscure. As the archetypal poet, he understands the source of poetic inspiration and is a prophet and a visionary. He is not confined by the limits of space and time. Taliesin is also able to change his shape, transforming himself not only into animals, but also into inanimate objects, such as a sword, a bridge, a spark or a coracle on the sea. There is also a certain heroic element in his character. Marged Haycock comments that 'the chief advantage of the existence of such a multifaceted character as Taliesin is that he is a convenient focus for so many varied traditions.'[46]

The folk tale about the poet, which is known variously as *Hanes Taliesin, Chwedl Taliesin* and *Ystoria Taliesin* (the story or legend of Taliesin), had not yet developed at the time when the poems in *Llyfr Taliesin* were composed.[47] It was from this source that Rhys Jones drew the poem that he included in his eighteenth-century anthology. The earliest surviving version of the legend is in the wonderful rag-bag of material gathered by Elis Gruffydd (c.1490-c.1552), usually known as 'the soldier of Calais' (where he spent a substantial part of his life as a member of the garrison). Another version of the story was recorded by the copyist John Jones of Gellilyfdy (c.1607). The legend was a staple of Welsh storytelling in Elis Gruffydd's day and remains so even today.

The hero of the story begins his life as Gwion Bach, a poor boy from Llanfair Caereinion, a few miles south west of Meifod. The witch Ceridwen and her bald husband Tegid have a hideous son called Morfran. In order to improve the boy's prospects in life, Ceridwen prepares a magic potion. It is made in a huge cauldron, which has to be kept boiling for a year and a day. At the end of that time there will be three drops of liquid left and whoever drinks them will gain all knowledge and learning and become the greatest poet of all. Ceridwen hires a blind man named Morda to keep the fire going and stir the cauldron. He uses the little boy Gwion Bach to act as his eyes and lead him around.

By the end of the year Ceridwen feels so tired that she cannot avoid going to sleep. But before she dozes off, she puts her unspeakably ugly son in the exact spot where the three amazing drops will drip into his mouth. As soon as Ceridwen begins to snore, Gwion Bach pushes the hapless Morfran out of the way and takes his place. The three drops of liquid suddenly splash out of the cauldron and land on Gwion's finger. They are boiling hot and he automatically puts his finger in his mouth, swallowing the drops. Only a poisonous residue is now left in the cauldron, which splits in two with a terrible scream. The magic drops give Gwion knowledge of everything that has been, everything that is, and everything that is to come. Aware of the danger threatening him, he runs away.

Ceridwen wakes up. A tearful Morfran tells her what has happened. Filled with rage she sets off to find the boy who has destroyed her son's future. Gwion Bach changes into a hare in order to outrun her. Ceridwen transforms herself into a greyhound to catch up with him. The boy jumps into the river, becoming a fish. The witch turns into an otter. Gwion surfaces and makes himself into a bird. Ceridwen pursues him as a hawk. Gwion spots a heap of threshed wheat on a barn floor and changes himself into a grain of wheat. Ceridwen finally becomes a hen, trampling the wheat until she finds Gwion Bach and swallows him.

Nine months go by and Gwion is re-born as Ceridwen's child. He is such a beautiful baby that she cannot bring herself to kill him or allow anyone else to kill him in her presence. So she sews a tiny coracle, carefully making sure that it is waterproof, puts the baby in it and lets it float away. Elffin, the wildly extravagant son of a man named Gwyddno, comes across the little coracle in his father's fish weir. When he sees the face of the three-day-old baby the young man exclaims *"Dyna dal iesin"* ("That's a beautiful forehead.") *"Taliesin bid"* ("Let it be Taliesin") answers the infant, and thereafter that is his name. When Taliesin grows older, Elffin finds himself in trouble because of some rash remarks that he has made at the court of Maelgwn Gwynedd. Taliesin rescues his patron, putting Maelgwn Gwynedd's twenty-four poets in their place in the process.

Included in the story are several poems ascribed to the legendary Taliesin, among them the verses that Rhys Jones printed in his collection. The 'author' of that poem reflects the characteristics of the mythical figure described by Marged Haycock in her study of *Llyfr Taliesin*. He is bombastic and boastful. He has been present at events derived from pre-Christian Welsh mythology, the Classical traditions of Greece and Rome and the Old and New Testaments. He is even prepared to state that he was in the manger at Bethlehem and on the cross with Christ.[48]

This might seem, on the face of it, a rather bizarre and offensive form of blasphemy. In fact it is an expression of what the poet's craft is meant to achieve. The poet can choose a time or a place and, through the power of his imagination and use of imagery and patterned words, can take you there. If he succeeds in what he is attempting to do, both the poet and his audience will indeed visit Africa or the ruins of Troy or Arianrhod's Fortress. They may even be present at Absalom's death or in the Bethlehem stable or on the cross of Calvary.

There is a parallel here with the sacramental mystery at the heart of Christian worship. The celebration of the Eucharist or Mass or Lord's Supper is often portrayed as a special type of remembering which transcends space and time so that those taking part are present at the events which they remember – or at least it is as if they were present there.

The story of Gwyddfarch and Tysilio and their vision of Rome on the mound of Meifod comes from the same thought-world as the tale of Taliesin. The holy men's experience transcends the limitations of nature in a way that parallels the poet's transcendence of space and time. The legend of the two early saints was no doubt influenced by the same type of myth-making process that transformed Cynan Garwyn's skilfully sycophantic court poet into a mysterious shape-shifting possessor of all knowledge. The result was a view of reality in which it was indeed possible to be in Rome and Meifod at one and the same time through a powerful act of imagining.

In the life of Tysilio the imagining was the result of a night of intense prayer and vigil rather than the product of poetic inspiration. The vision is portrayed as his personal gift to Gwyddfarch, the abbot who had been his spiritual friend and guide and who had ensured his safety when he turned his back on Brochwel's court. Gwyddfarch had been the one who led Tysilio towards his calling. Tysilio was the one who helped Gwyddfarch fulfil his final ambition. This touching example of soul friendship doubtless reflects the ideals of the storyteller and his milieu. We have no way of knowing if it bears any relationship to the actual life and thought of the earliest Christian community at Meifod.

NOTES

[1] For the foundation of Ystrad Marchell see *The Charters of the Abbey of Ystrad Marchell*, edited by Graham C.G. Thomas (Aberystwyth, 1997), pp.10-12. For its suppression see David H. Williams, *The Welsh Cistercians*, 2 vols (Caldey Island, Tenby, 1984), I, 106; *The Cistercian Abbeys: Far from the Concourse of Men*, edited by David Robinson (London, 1998), p.180 and Thomas, *Charters*, p.51.

[2] James Edward McGoldrick, *Luther's English Connection* (Milwaukee, 1979), pp.11-14.

[3] A detailed and vivid portrait of Robert ap Rhys is given by Glanmor Williams, *The Welsh Church from Conquest to Reformation* (Cardiff, 1976), pp.322-7.

[4] Williams, *Welsh Church*, p.520.

[5] Thomas, *Charters*, p.238.

[6] *Gwaith Cynddelw Brydydd Mawr*, 2 vols, edited by Nerys Ann Jones and Ann Parry Owen (Cardiff 1991-5), I, 29-30.

[7] S. Baring-Gould and John Fisher, *The Lives of the British Saints*, 4 vols (London, 1907-13) III, 219-20; Peter C. Bartrum, *A Welsh Classical Dictionary: People in History and Legend up to about A.D. 1000* (Aberystwyth, 1993), pp.344-5; Gilbert H. Doble, *The Saints of Cornwall, Part Five: Saints of Mid-Cornwall* (Oxford, 1970), pp.106-11 (a translation of Albert Le Grand, 'The Life of Saint Suliau or Syliau').

[8] D.R. Thomas, *The History of the Diocese of St Asaph*, 3 vols (Oswestry, 1908-13), I, 496-7.

[9] For Pennant Melangell see *The Montgomeryshire Collections,* LXXXII (1994), which includes articles on the parish, the church and Melangell and her shrine, among them H. Pryce, 'A New Edition of the *Historia Divae Monacella*' (pp.23-40).

[10] Bartrum, *Welsh Classical Dictionary,* p.60 ('Brochwel Ysgithrog, king of Powys').

[11] Thomas Pennant, *Tours in Wales,* edited by John Rhys, 3 vols (Caernarfon, 1883), III, 163.

[12] Huw Pryce, *Native Law and the Church in Medieval Wales* (Oxford, 1993), p.202.

[13] On the link between virginity and feminine sanctity and the significance of the hare hiding under Melangell's skirt see Jane Cartwright, *Y Forwyn Fair, Santesau a Lleianod: Agweddau ar Wyryfdod a Diweirdeb yng Nghymru'r Oesoedd Canol* (Cardiff, 1999), pp.115-17.

[14] In Albert Le Grand's narrative, Tysilio is called Suliau, Brochwel is Brocmail and Gwyddfarch is Guymarchus. I have retained the Welsh names.

[15] Waldo Williams, *Cerddi* (Newtown, 1992), p.102.

[16] Ifor Williams, *Canu Llywarch Hen* (Cardiff, 1970), pp.1-32; Jenny Rowland, *Early Welsh Saga Poetry: A Study and Edition of the Englynion* (Cambridge, 1990), pp.7-73, 404-18, 468-76.

[17] *The Beginnings of Welsh Poetry: Studies by Sir Ifor Williams,* edited by Rachel Bromwich (Cardiff, 1980), p.137.

[18] *Llyfr Du Caerfyrddin,* edited by A.O.H. Jarman (Cardiff, 1982), pp.62-5, 112; Williams, *Canu Llywarch Hen,* pp.27-9, 176; Ifor Williams, *Lectures on Early Welsh Poetry* (Dublin, 1970), pp.14-16; Kenneth Jackson, *Early Welsh Gnomic Poems* (Cardiff, 1973), pp.18-20, 45; Rowland, *Early Welsh Saga Poetry,* pp.229-40.

[19] Thomas Gwynn Jones, *Y Dwymyn 1934-35* (Cardiff, 1972), pp.19-35.

[20] Jones, *Y Dwymyn,* p.22.

[21] Jones, *Y Dwymyn,* p.23.

[22] Jones, *Y Dwymyn,* pp.24-5.

[23] Jones, *Y Dwymyn,* p.26.

[24] Jones, *Y Dwymyn,* p.26.

[25] Jones, *Y Dwymyn,* p.32.

[26] Jones, *Y Dwymyn,* p.34.

[27] Jones, *Y Dwymyn,* p.36.

[28] *Gwaith Cynddelw Brydydd Mawr,* I, 15-52. However Nerys Ann Jones and Morfydd E.Owen, 'Twelfth-century Welsh hagiography: the *Gogynfeirdd* poems to saints' in *Celtic Hagiography and Saints' Cults,* edited by Jane Cartwright (Cardiff, 2003), pp.45-76 (pp.59-61), now suggest that Cynddelw's poem may been 'composed as a response to a political crisis'. The death of Madog ap Maredudd and his heir Llywelyn led to a power struggle in southern Powys in the early 1160s. The protagonists were Owain Fychan and his cousin Owain Cyfeiliog. Jones and Owen interpret the poem as an appeal on behalf of the Meifod community to Owain Gwynedd to intervene and resolve the conflict.

[29] *Brut y Tywysogyon or The Chronicle of the Princes: Peniarth MS 20 Version,* translated by Thomas Jones (Cardiff, 1952), pp.1, 4-6, 8.

[30] Marged Haycock, *Blodeugerdd Barddas o Ganu Crefyddol Cynnar* (Llandybie, 1994), pp. 274-6.

[31] Doble, *Saints of Mid-Cornwall*, p.108.

[32] Baring-Gould and Fisher, *Lives of the British Saints*, IV, 297-8.

[33] *Gwaith Cynddelw Brydydd Mawr*, I, 32.

[34] Ifor Williams, *Pedeir Keinc y Mabinogi* (Cardiff, 1964), pp.8-13.

[35] Rhys Jones, *Gorchestion Beirdd Cymru: neu Flodau Godidowgrwydd Awen* (Shrewsbury, 1773), pp.7-8.

[36] Jones, *Gorchestion*, p.5.

[37] Ifor Williams, *Canu Taliesin* (Cardiff, 1960), pp.xxxix-xl.

[38] Bartrum, *Welsh Classical Dictionary*, p. 167 ('Cynan Garwyn ap Brochwel Ysgithrog ap Cyngen') and pp.73-4 ('Cadell Ddyrnllug').

[39] Williams, *Canu Taliesin*, p.1.

[40] Bartrum, *Welsh Classical Dictionary*, pp.632-4 ('Urien Rheged ap Cynfarch Oer'); Nora Chadwick, *The British Heroic Age: The Welsh and the Men of the North* (Cardiff, 1976), pp.102-4.

[41] Williams, *Canu Taliesin*, p.6.

[42] Williams, *Canu Taliesin*, p.12.

[43] Williams, *Canu Taliesin*, pp.13-16.

[44] Williams, *Canu Taliesin*, pp.xvii-xviii; Roger White and Philip Barker, *Wroxeter: Life and Death of a Roman City* (Stroud, 1998), p.132.

[45] Marged Haycock, 'Llyfr Taliesin: Astudiaethau ar rai agweddau', Ph.D. thesis (University of Wales, Aberystwyth, 1982).

[46] Haycock, 'Llyfr Taliesin', pp.53-8.

[47] Haycock, 'Llyfr Taliesin', p.58. For the legend of Taliesin see Ifor Williams, *Chwedl Taliesin* (Cardiff, 1957) and *Ystoria Taliesin*, edited by Patrick K. Ford (Cardiff, 1992).

[48] Jones, *Gorchestion*, p.7.

2. CYNDDYLAN AND HELEDD

i) Beuno and the Hunter

Albert Le Grand tells us that Gwyddfarch fell ill some time after he and Tysilio had shared their vision of Rome on the hillock at Meifod. Realising that he did not have long to live, the old abbot called his monks together. He recommended to them that they choose Tysilio as his successor. This they did. The erstwhile prince remained abbot of Meifod until his deceased brother's wife tried to coerce him into leaving the monastery and marrying her. She had assumed the throne on her husband's death, but had promised the important men of Powys that she would make Tysilio her consort because he was the last remaining member of her late husband's family (their marriage had been childless). Tysilio refused and the angry princess proceeded to persecute his community, depriving it of its income. Tysilio left Meifod for his former island refuge in the Menai Straits. Then, when even that did not appease the angry widow, he set sail for Brittany, where he founded a new monastery.

The scorned princess eventually died and the community at Meifod sent two of their oldest monks to invite Tysilio to come home. The Breton monks refused to allow their abbot to leave them. Tysilio shut himself in the monastery church to pray that God's will in this matter might be revealed. When he emerged, he told the brethren that he now knew that he did not have very long left to live and therefore that it would be better for him to stay in Brittany. However, to make up for the Meifod monks' disappointment, he sent them the gospel book which he had always carried with him and the staff which he used when travelling. Then Tysilio died and was buried, according to Albert, in the church of his abbey of Saint-Suliau-sur-Rance, not far from Saint-Malo.

From a historical point of view, the story about Tysilio's clash with his sister-in-law is pure invention.[1] According to Albert, the name of Brochwel's short-lived successor was Jacob (Iago). He reigned for only two years, leaving behind him the widow who then ascended the throne and pursued his brother the abbot. In reality Brochwel was succeeded by a son named Cynan Garwyn, the patron of the historical Taliesin. Cynan reigned for a considerable time. He was followed by his son Selyf Sarffgadau ('Selyf Serpent of Battles'), who died at the battle of Chester which probably took place in 616.[2] The imaginary tale of Tysilio and his sister-in-law was doubtless intended to explain how Tysilio of Meifod came to be regarded as the founder of a community in Britanny.

While Tysilio was still abbot of Meifod, he was visited by Beuno, a fellow native of Powys who was destined to become one of the principal religious figures of Gwynedd. A Welsh life of Beuno is included in *Llyfr Ancr Llanddewibrefi* ('The Book of the Anchorite of Llanddewibrefi'), a manuscript which was compiled in 1346.[3] It informs us that Beuno was the son of an elderly gentleman named Bugi and his wife Beren, who lived at Banhenig near the river Severn. The genealogy at the end of the life suggests that Bugi was one of the Cadelling, the descendants of Cadell Ddyrnllug, the reputed founder of the principal princely family of early Powys. Medieval tradition thus regarded him as a relative of Brochwel Ysgithrog, Tysilio and Cynan Garwyn. This may throw some light on the life's portrayal of Beuno's rather complex dealings with Cynan and his family.

Baring-Gould and Fisher offer two possible sites for Beuno's birthplace. One is Trelystan near Welshpool, where there is a place called Badnage (formerly Badnich) Wood. Trelystan is some way from the river Severn but is very close to a Roman Road. Their second and preferred suggestion is further north at Llanymynech, a village which is actually on the river Vyrnwy, but where there is a holy well dedicated to St Benion or Bennion. Gwallter Mechain, the nineteenth century antiquary and poet, claimed somewhat improbably that, although the obvious translation of the parish's name is 'village of the monks', it should really be translated 'village of the miners'. If the link with Beuno is correct, the 'mynech' of the parish name may refer to him and his followers. [4]

According to the life, Beuno was sent south to be educated at Caerwent. His teacher was Tangusius, who was probably the abbot of the monastery there. After he had learned to read the Scriptures and recite church services, Beuno was ordained. Ynyr Gwent, the local ruler, became his disciple and gave him land in Ewyas (now part of Herefordshire). There is still a Llanfeuno in the area. Bugi was taken ill and messengers were sent to Beuno to ask him to come home and give his father his blessing. The holy man left three of his followers in Ewyas and travelled back to Banhenig. There he administered the last rites to his father and Bugi died.

Beuno stayed in his father's township for some time and built a church there. He also planted an acorn on the edge of his father's grave. The author of the life tells us that the acorn grew into an enormous oak tree. It had a long branch which formed an arch. If an Englishman went under the arch he would die. If a Welshman went under it he would come to no harm.[5] This fear and hatred of the English who were about to threaten Beuno's native area is something that will surface again in the life. It may well reflect the hagiographer's own prejudices rather than those of Beuno himself.

Beuno acquired a new patron. Mawn was a son of Brochwel Ysgithrog and the brother of St Tysilio of Meifod and Cynan Garwyn, prince of Powys.[6] He gave Aberriw (Berriew) on the banks of the river Severn to God and Beuno in exchange for his prayers. A rough standing stone by the ancient lane that leads from Berriew towards the river Severn is known as Maen Beuno. D.R. Thomas suggests that the stone marks the boundary of the land that Mawn granted to Beuno and that it may also be the spot where he began to teach the people of the area.[7]

One day Beuno was walking along the banks of the river Severn towards the ford when he heard a voice drifting over from the far bank. A hunter had come across a hare and was urging his hounds to chase it. Instead of using familiar Welsh words he shouted something at the dogs in a foreign language. The stranger was an Englishman. Beuno's reaction was immediate. He went straight back to his community and told his monks to get dressed, put on their shoes and prepare to leave as soon as possible.

According to the hagiographer, Beuno seems to have gone into a state of complete panic. He wanted to put as much space between himself and the newcomer as he could. He told his startled followers that the man came from an abominable nation that spoke a strange tongue. The presence of the hunter on the far bank of the river was a sign that the invaders had arrived and they were the sort of people who would hang on to whatever they got hold of. The monks therefore had to leave Berriew. One disciple was chosen to remain behind there. Beuno blessed this brave soul and presented him with a cross. Apparently it had been carved by the abbot himself.

The band of monks headed north to Tysilio's monastery at Meifod. There they spent a symbolic forty days and forty nights. Beuno needed the support of another important man. Perhaps it was Tysilio who suggested his brother Cynan Garwyn, prince of Powys. At first Cynan granted Beuno some land for yet another church at Meifod. But it must soon have become clear that two major figures like Tysilio and Beuno needed plenty of breathing space. So Cynan gave Beuno more land a reasonable distance away from Meifod, this time at Gwyddelwern – a place with a name that means 'the Irishman's alders'. The Irishman was said to have been Llorcan Wyddel, one of those whom Beuno is reputed to have raised from the dead.

At last the restless abbot seemed to have found a secure spiritual home far from any threat of an English invasion. Then suddenly something went terribly wrong. Cynan's grandsons (mistakenly called 'nephews' by the author of the life), the sons of Selyf 'Serpent of Battles', were hunting in the area. They arrived at Beuno's monastery and demanded food. Beuno told his servants to take a young ox from the mountain pasture, kill it, cook it and serve it to the lively young men. They duly brought the animal and butchered it, putting the meat in a large cooking pot with a blazing fire beneath it. The hours went by. The servants continued to feed the fire beneath the cooking pot with fuel. But all their efforts were in vain. The water in the cooking pot refused to boil and the meat remained the same colour as when it had first been put in.

The huntsmen, deprived of their meal, got more and more frustrated and angry. One of them rashly suggested that it was all Beuno's fault. The abbot must be using some of his special powers to make sure that the water wouldn't boil and that the young men went hungry. Unfortunately Beuno, who seems to have had a savage temper, overheard the remark. He cursed the young man who had made it. Before the end of the day the critic had become a corpse. The others also became the victims of Beuno's wrath. He reminded them that everything he possessed had been given freely to him and God by their grandfather. The young noblemen didn't have an automatic right to claim food and shelter from him, as they did from their grandfather's lay subjects. Beuno then pronounced a curse on the royal family of Powys, asking God to ensure that their relatives never possessed the land and that they might lose both their earthly and their eternal inheritance.

After this inflammatory episode Beuno left Gwyddelwern and moved to the banks of the river Dee, looking for land on which he could build yet another church. But it was still Cynan Garwyn's territory and the prince must have heard of the awful doom that Beuno had decreed for the royal house of Powys. The prince refused to assist the holy man, who was forced to move on into Flintshire. There he was given a grant of land by one of Cynan Garwyn's more congenial grandsons, Tyfid the son of Eliudd, Selyf's brother. According to a medieval Welsh genealogy, Tyfid's wife Gwenlo was Beuno's sister, which may explain his friendly attitude towards the itinerant holy man.[8] Beuno built yet another church in Tyfid's territory.

Tyfid and Gwenlo were attending a service in that church when one of the most dramatic and colourful incidents in Welsh religious folklore took place. Gwenfrewi, the couple's beautiful unmarried daughter, had been left at home to keep an eye on things. A young nobleman of royal blood named Caradog came past and stopped at the house to ask for a drink. Gwenfrewi brought it to him and he took a violent fancy to her. She refused to give in to him and managed to make her escape, running away towards Beuno's church. Caradog got back on his horse and rode after her. He was so angry that when he caught up with her at the entrance to the church, he drew his sword and cut off her head. Beuno was drawn to the door by the commotion and saw what happened. He immediately cursed Caradog. The young man melted like wax, forming a pool on the ground. Beuno put Gwenfrewi's head back on her body, which was lying on the threshold of the church. Then he finished celebrating mass, and at the end of the service the girl stood up again restored to life. A spring gushed forth from the ground that had been stained with her blood. This was to become Ffynnon Wenfrewi or St Winifred's Well, an important place of pilgrimage.[9]

Beuno's travels were still not at end. Cadwallon, the son of Cadfan and one of Cynan Garwyn's daughters, became ruler of Gwynedd. Beuno decided to move to the new king's territory, thus retreating even further away from the threat of the encroaching English. According to his hagiographer, Beuno was granted some land in Arfon by Cadwallon. In exchange the holy man gave the king a golden sceptre that he himself had been given by Cynan Garwyn just before the latter's death. The sceptre's value was the equivalent of sixty cows. Beuno duly started to build a church with an enclosure around it.

One day he and his disciples were busy working on the wall when a woman approached them carrying a newborn baby. She asked Beuno to bless the infant. The holy man told her to wait until he and his monks had finished their work. But the child began to cry so loudly that it was impossible to concentrate on anything. Beuno asked the mother why the baby was making so much noise. The woman replied that the land on which the abbot was building his church really belonged to the child's father. Beuno was horrified to hear this. He told his followers to stop work immediately. The infant was baptised and then they all set out together to visit Cadwallon at the royal court. They wanted to find out why he had given Beuno someone else's land. The king was not impressed by this delegation. He would not give any explanation for his behaviour and said that he was not prepared to give Beuno another gift of land to replace the one that he was occupying at present. He also refused to return the golden sceptre, saying that he had given it to someone else. Beuno was furious and, in characteristic fashion, cursed Cadwallon, asking God to make sure that the king would soon be deprived of all his territory.

Cadwallon was one of the great heroic figures of early Welsh history and tradition. According to the medieval hagiographer, the ruler of Gwynedd does not seem to have been unnerved by the saint's curse. The king's cousin, Gwyddaint, was a rather more sensitive soul. He went out to look for Beuno and found him sitting brooding on a stone by the river. Gwyddaint quickly patched things up between the royal family and the outraged holy man. He gave his own township of Clynnog to God and Beuno in return for the abbot's prayers for the souls of his cousin Cadwallon and himself. Beuno was satisfied. The curse was revoked. At last the wandering abbot had found a place where he could settle permanently. Beuno's community at Clynnog Fawr in Arfon was to become one of the major religious centres in north-west Wales.

The final section of the life recounts two more incidents in which Beuno brought decapitated people back to life. One of them was a princess named Tegiwg, the daughter of the saint's former patron, Ynyr Gwent. The other was Tegiwg's husband and murderer, Cadwallon's steward. He had had his head cut off by Iddon, Tegiwg's brother, as an act of revenge. The outraged king of Gwynedd had threatened to kill Iddon unless Beuno restored life to the dead man. Beuno did so, earning an apology and another grant of land from Cadwallon.

The Beuno portrayed in the life is a strange, temperamental, semi-mythological figure. On the one hand he deals out powerfully destructive curses, on the other he gains a reputation for raising the dead to life (particularly if they have been decapitated). He has a phobia about the English, realising the threat that they represent to the remaining Welsh kingdoms, but he also has a love-hate relationship with the Welsh rulers who become his patrons. Some of these characteristics may of course stem from the particular agenda of the unidentified Welsh ecclesiastic who wrote the life.[10] The defence of the lands and privileges of church institutions threatened by greedy or arrogant secular rulers is easier if they are linked to a saint who is known to be able to curse his enemies with devastating results – and who has a particular reputation for putting royalty in their place. The gentler side of Beuno may have been useful in persuading pilgrims to visit Clynnog Fawr and his other churches. The poets began to speak of Beuno as someone who had raised at least six (and possibly seven) people from the dead.[11] Such a spiritual patron was an obvious person to turn to in times of acute spiritual and personal crisis.

However the marked antipathy towards the English attributed to Beuno by his hagiographer echoes the conflicts that developed during the saint's lifetime. Selyf 'Serpent of Battles', the prince whose sons offended Beuno and were cursed by him, was killed while leading the men of Powys against the pagan Northumbrian king Aethelfrith at Chester in about 616. In Welsh tradition the battle was known as *Gwaith Perllan Fangor* ('the Action of Bangor Orchard'). Bede records that twelve hundred unarmed monks from the monastery of Bangor-Is-coed (Bangor-on-Dee) who had come out to pray for victory for the Britons/Welsh were massacred by the Northumbrians before the fighting began.[12]

The Welsh Triads list three 'Gate-Keepers' who apparently played a heroic part in what turned out to be a disastrous defeat for the Welsh. One of them comes from a later period and cannot have been present there. He was Gwgon Gleddyfrudd ('of the Red Sword'), king of Ceredigion, a noted warrior who was also described in the Triads as one of the three 'Slaughter-Blocks' of the Island of Britain. He rode a horse called Bucheslom and had a daughter who was one of the legendary beauties with whom medieval Welsh poets would compare their girlfriends. Gwgon was drowned in 871. The other two figures almost certainly did take part in the battle. They were members of subsidiary ruling families from Powys: Madog son of Rhun, and Gwion son of Cyndrwyn. Gwion's father came from Llystynwynnan which was probably near Moel Feliarth in the parish of Llangadfan, west of Llanfair Caereinion. Cyndrwyn's other children included Cynddylan and Heledd, who were to become the subject of the most tragic of the sagas of Powys.[13]

Around the same time that they defeated Selyf at Chester, the Northumbrians snuffed out the little kingdom of Elmet (Elfed) around Leeds and the Welsh/Britons lost their last foothold east of the Pennines. In 617 Edwin killed Aethelfrith and became king of Northumbria. Around 628 he invaded Anglesey, blockading Cadwallon in Ynys Lannog (Priestholm or Puffin Island). Cadwallon was forced to take refuge in Ireland for a time. If, as has been suggested, Beuno died around the year 630, he must have been almost within earshot of the alien tongue of the Northumbrian invaders during his final days. After a brief exile Cadwallon returned and counter-attacked.

A ninth or tenth-century poem claims that Cadwallon used the hill-fort on Cefn Digoll to the east of Welshpool as his base and fought seven battles a day from there for seven months.[14] The Triads record one of these battles as one of the 'Three Defilements of the Severn'. The compiler of the Triad claims that the slaughter was so great when Cadwallon and his warriors clashed with Edwin's English army that the river was polluted from its source to its mouth. There is some literary evidence that the king of Gwynedd had the support of the men of Powys in this fighting that took place in what was still the heart of their territory.[15]

Cadwallon formed an alliance with Penda of Mercia and invaded Northumbria. They defeated and killed Edwin in 633 and the remnants of his army disintegrated. Northumbria, united by Edwin, now divided again into its two original kingdoms of Bernicia and Deira. Neither of their rulers lasted long. Within a few months both Osric of Deira and Eanfrith of Bernicia had been eliminated. The Northumbrians' remaining hopes rested on Oswald, the new king of Bernicia. In 634 his small army met that of Cadwallon near Hexham. Oswald, the Northumbrian Christian who was later to be regarded as a saint, set up a huge wooden cross before the battle and prayed to God for his assistance. By the end of the day Oswald was victorious and Cadwallon, the British Christian, lay dead on the battlefield. Penda, the pagan, slipped away, returning to Mercia to strengthen his power base there.

Eight years later Oswald himself was killed at a battle known by the Welsh as Gwaith Gogwy and by the Northumbrian historian Bede as Maserfelth. The site of the battle has traditionally been identified as Oswestry, although recently it has been suggested that it might have been Makerfield near Wigan.[16] Oswald had apparently been attempting to destroy an alliance between Powys and the Mercians. Bede (who had a profound dislike of the Welsh) doesn't even mention that they were present. The poets of Powys however regarded Gwaith Gogwy as a major victory. One of them noted that Cynddylan son of Cyndrwyn was among the leaders of the men of Powys in the battle, while Cynddelw Brydydd Hir imagined St Tysilio in heaven urging his countrymen on to victory.[17]

ii) The Land of Cynddylan

If the oak tree that Beuno planted on his father's grave really was at Llanymynech, it has a certain symbolic significance. The tree, we are told, could differentiate between the Welsh and the English with deadly effect. Llanymynech itself represents a dividing line. Part of the village is in Powys and part of the village in Shropshire. But borders are not always definitive. They can and do move. There was a time when most, if not all, of Shropshire was part of Powys and its ruler was Cynddylan ap Cyndrwyn.

It is now thought that Powys in the early seventh century was probably some type of confederation in which a prince or king was acknowledged as overlord by several subsidiary rulers. The dominant ruling family was the Cadelling, the family that traced its origins to Cadell Ddyrnllug and that included Brochwel Ysgithrog, Cynan Garwyn and Selyf 'Serpent of Battles'. They were the overall rulers of Powys. One subsidiary family was the Cyndrwynyn from the Caereinion area. They do not seem to have been related to the Cadelling, and may have owed their advancement to military prowess and political manoeuvring. Cynddylan ap Cyndrwyn may have come into prominence as the result of some kind of power vacuum after the death of Selyf at the battle of Chester. [18]

He became responsible for the area of Powys that had its capital at Pengwern, possibly on the banks of the river Severn. Giraldus Cambrensis (Gerallt Gymro), writing in the twelfth century, was convinced that the site of Pengwern was where Shrewsbury Castle stood in his own time.[19] Later antiquaries suggested that Old St Chad's Church had been built in the place where the princes of Powys had once held court. As has been mentioned earlier, the most recent tendency is to locate Cynddylan's court at the Berth, an Iron Age fort among the lakes and marshes north of Baschurch in Shropshire. His territory would have extended as far as the river Tern and included the former Roman town at Wroxeter and the Wrekin and the Ercall, hills which jut out of the Shropshire plain.[20]

There are two sources for our information about Cynddylan. The earliest is a lament that dates from the seventh century and thus is almost contemporary with its subject. The second is the collection of poems known as *Canu Heledd*. It is generally agreed that this second group of poems was once part of a saga telling the story of Cynddylan and his sister Heledd, the prose sections of which have not survived. The poetry dates from the ninth or tenth century. The events that they purport to describe took place two or three hundred years before.[21]

There is some disagreement about the background to the earlier poem. It has generally been assumed that Cynddylan was killed during a border skirmish with the Mercians. The elegy implies that he died while trying to steal (or possibly defend) cattle at an unidentified place called Penawg (Pennog) and this is the view accepted by R. Geraint Gruffydd in his detailed study of it:

> I lost a brave unyielding merciless man
> When he took the cattle of Pennog.
> He raided across Tren to the arrogant country.
> I shall lament until I am in the unmoving earth
> Because of the killing of Cynddylan of dear fame.[22]

Jenny Rowland has however suggested that Cynddylan might have been one of Penda of Mercia's Welsh allies in his final campaign against Oswiu

(Oswy) of Bernicia in 655. This ended in disaster. Penda and all the Welsh/British kings taking part were killed. If Cynddylan was in their number, he earned an honourable death, in contrast to the fate of Cadafael of Gwynedd. Cadafael lost his nerve before the battle and slipped off home with his men. As a result he was nicknamed the 'Battle Refuser' and regarded with contempt.

The seventh-century lament would seem to show that there was some tension or hostility between Cynddylan's followers (including the author of the poem) and the Cadelling, the overlords of Powys. It also reveals that Cynddylan was engaged in raids beyond the border of his territory. In eastern Powys in the early seventh century that border was marked by the Shropshire river Tren (now Tern). Beyond it was the *tir trahawg* ('arrogant country') of Mercia. Cynddylan's adventures included an incursion into South Wales to steal cattle from the meadows beside the river Taf. Rather more expected is a reference to a ferocious battle at Caerlwytgoed (Lichfield). Their enemy there seem to have been fellow Christians. The poem refers to an archbishop and his *myneich llyfr afael* ('book-clutching monks') whose influence was unable to protect their warriors or prevent the Powys men from seizing large numbers of horses and cattle.

> Greatness in battle. Morial took
> Many possessions in front of Caerlwytgoed.
> Fifteen hundred cattle at the end of the fighting,
> Eighty horses and the same number of harnesses,
> The wretched archbishop in a cloak with corners,
> And the book-clutching monks did not defend them.[23]

The identity of these monks and their archbishop has been the source of some debate. They are unlikely to have been Saxon Christians. Bede gives the impression that missionary work in Mercia did not start until after Penda's death in 655. St Chad did not establish his see at Lichfield until after he had been consecrated as Bishop of the Mercians in 669. It did not become a Saxon archbishopric until 787. Cynddylan's opponents may perhaps have been a residual community of British Christians who had survived the invasion and come to terms with their new Mercian neighbours. There is a possibility that the Welsh raiders regarded them as quislings who had sold out by collaborating with the enemy and therefore deserved no sympathy or mercy. Jenny Rowland however suggests that the reference may be either to the clerics accompanying a Northumbrian army advancing through Mercia or to the fact that the prayers of their archbishop and monks back home in Northumbria did not protect their warriors during their invasion. This may also reflect a feeling that the 'book-clutching monks' of Northumbria regarded themselves as superior to the religious of the Welsh/British church.[24]

There are a few lines in the seventh-century elegy that hint at themes which would be developed a couple of centuries later in the Heledd saga. They tell us that Cynddylan was a young, unmarried man and that the whereabouts of his grave seems to be unknown. Perhaps the poet's most telling remark is that 'a brother did not escape to his sister from the battle.' This certainly sounds like a reference to Cynddylan's relationship with his sister Heledd. Jenny Rowland suggests that the last two lines of the poem may be corrupt or interpolated.[25] They talk about the author's sense of guilt, which is also a strong strand in the Heledd poems. In the elegy the poet does not think that he will be brought to God's judgement, but still confesses that no one has committed a sin like the one of which he himself is guilty.

The elegy that was almost certainly written not long after Cynddylan's death does not convey the sense of overwhelming tragedy that is evident in the later Heledd cycle. The lament is for a brave border raider with a gift for fighting. There is no expression of concern about the Mercians pouring across the Shropshire plain and looting and burning on the way, while leaving a trail of corpses in their wake. It may be that the poem was composed just after the death of Cynddylan and just before the Mercians turned on eastern Powys. Wendy Davies notes that Penda's descendants were in control of the area around the Wrekin by the late seventh century.[26] Whether Cynddylan was killed in a fight over cattle at Pennog or in a distant battle at Winwaed, his death seems to have given the Mercians an opportunity to take over his territory.

Giraldus was still expressing a nostalgic sadness at the loss of eastern Powys in the twelfth century. It is thus hardly surprising that the poets and storytellers of Powys soon managed to transform the loss of the Shropshire plain into a tragic saga. Cynddylan became an even greater hero than his original elegist had managed to make him, while the heart-rending poetry put in the mouth of his sister Heledd contains what are

still some of the most starkly beautiful and powerful verses in the Welsh
language:

Cynddylan's hall is dark tonight,
No fire, no bed,
I'll weep for a while, and then be silent.

Cynddylan's hall is dark tonight,
No fire, no candle.
Who except God will keep me sane?

Cynddylan's hall is dark tonight,
No fire, no light.
A longing for you comes over me.

Cynddylan's hall has a dark ceiling,
After fair companionship.
Pity the one who doesn't do the good he has a chance to do.

Cynddylan's hall, you look feeble now,
Your shield is in a grave,
While he was alive, no one could breach the gate.

Cynddylan's hall, so remote tonight
After what happened to you.
Death, why do you leave me here?

Cynddylan's hall is comfortless tonight
On a rock of affliction:
No strong lord, no battle host, no sanctuary.

Cynddylan's hall is dark tonight,
No fire, no songs.
Tears of affliction mark both cheeks.

Cynddylan's hall is dark tonight,
No fire, no heroes.
My tears keep on flowing.

Cynddylan's hall, I'm pierced through as I see it:
No roof, no fire.
My lord is dead: I am still living.

Cynddylan's hall is so ruined tonight
After brave warriors:
Elfan, Cynddylan, Caeog.

Cynddylan's hall is in pain tonight –
After the respect that adorned me:
No men, no women kept it.

Cynddylan's hall is quiet tonight
Having lost its bravest.
Merciful God, what shall I do?

Cynddylan's has a dark ceiling
After the Englishmen destroyed
Cynddylan and Elfan Powys.

Cynddylan's hall is dark tonight
Around Cyndrwyn's children:
Cynon and Gwion and Gwyn.

Cynddylan's hall, I'm pierced through every hour
Remembering joy and laughter
We shared together on your hearth.[27]

iii) The Tragedy of Heledd

The loss of eastern Powys was a blow that had a lasting resonance. Five hundred years later Powys was still described as having six hundreds (cantrefi). It was, however, noted that three of them were under Norman and English occupation and had become known as Shropshire.[28] In the eighth century the Mercian king Offa constructed a great dyke along the Welsh border, which remains a symbolic demarcation line between Wales and England. The creation of the saga of Heledd and Cynddylan in the middle of the ninth century may have been a reaction to this very visible attempt to cut the inhabitants of Powys off forever from territory that had once been theirs. Its composition may have been intended to fix the idea of the lost territory in the memory of the people of a diminished Powys, suggesting the possibility that, despite Offa's Dyke, the cantrefi beyond the new border might some day be regained. It may also have been meant as a warning to ensure that a terrible mistake from the past would not be repeated.

Powys certainly felt under pressure in the mid-ninth century. Cyngen had succeeded his father Cadell as its ruler in 808. He was attacked by the Mercians and overwhelmed. The *Brut* records that in 823 'the Saxons took the kingdom of Powys for their own.'[29] Somehow Cyngen seems to have won his kingdom back, and it may have been that achievement which led him to erect a pillar that can still be seen in Pant-y-Groes (Valle Crucis) in Iâl. The pillar commemorates his great-grandfather Elise, who had also succeeded in rescuing Powys from English domination around the year 725. Cyngen died in 855 and with him the dynasty of the Cadelling came to an end. Rhodri Mawr, king of Gwynedd, and son of Cyngen's sister Nest, added Powys to his domains.

The prose sections of the Heledd saga no longer exist, but it is clear from the poetry that remains that the princess was portrayed as being in some way responsible for what happened to her brother and his people.

In 1954 Glyn Jones and T. J. Morgan wrote an imaginative reconstruction of the Heledd Saga for a radio broadcast. It was entitled 'The Misfortunes of Princess Heledd' and was based on advice from Sir Ifor Williams, who had edited the original poems. Jones and Morgan suggested that a Saxon chieftain might have come to Cynddylan's court to ask for the hand of his sister Heledd in marriage. At the time Heledd was in mourning for her sister Ffreuer, who had died from the yellow plague. The bereaved princess was drowning her sorrows with copious quantities of red-black wine and behaving in a rather antisocial manner. She refused to meet the Saxon and dismissed his suit contemptuously. In a drunken rage she shouted abuse about the Mercians from her chamber window so that the visitors could hear it. She denounced the neighbouring people as abject cowards. Burning with anger the Saxon chieftain rode home. When he returned, he brought a Mercian army with him. They met Cynddylan's warriors at the town on the river Tren. Cynddylan and his brothers Elfan, Cynan and Gwyn were all killed in the fighting.[30]

In this attempt to recover the original story, Heledd's fatal weakness is seen as a combination of drunkenness and arrogance.[31] One series of *englynion* does indeed refer to Heledd's former enjoyment of copious quantities of mead. It begins:

Before I rested on the hard skin of a goat
Greedy for holly,
Bryn's mead made me drunk.

Before I rested on the hard skin of a goat,
A holly-loving goat
Tren's mead made me drunk.[32]

This may however be no more than a comparison of the miserable present with the joyful past. She may be thinking back to days of cheerful feasting and carousing with her brothers. Another possibility, particularly as Tren is the place of Cynddylan's death in the Heledd poems, is that the 'mead' referred to is Cynddylan's blood and the blood of a second hero or relative killed at Bryn. Heledd may metaphorically have become 'drunk' with sorrow before settling down to rest on her hard prickly goat's skin. There is certainly nothing to justify the suggestion that Ffreuer's death had suddenly driven her sister to start hitting the bottle.

Her song about Ffreuer is however one of the occasions on which Heledd admits that something that she had said was responsible for the disaster that has overtaken eastern Powys and the Cyndrwynyn, her family:

Ffreuer is fortunate, she has no pain tonight,
Having lost a host of warriors:
They died because of my tongue.[33]

Similarly as she watches Eglwysau Basa (now Baschurch in Shropshire), the religious centre of Cynddylan's kingdom, being destroyed, she confesses that her tongue has caused their destruction:

The Churches of Basa are crumbling tonight.
My tongue made it happen.
They are red, my sorrow is too great.[34]

In another verse she recalls:

I had brothers whom God took from me.
My misfortune made it happen.
They did not cheat their way to fame.[35]

The idea that Heledd's mistake was linked to a refusal to marry a leading Mercian does seem plausible. Her tragic flaw seems to have been *traha* – self-destructive pride. Her consciousness that she was one of the Cyndrwynyn, a princely Powys family, may have been at the root of the scorn that she felt for the pagan foreigners on the far side of the Tren. She clearly insulted someone in such a scathing and arrogant way that it led to the death of her brothers and the destruction of their kingdom:

Stop, maidens, stand and look
At Cynddylan's land.
The court of Pengwern is in flames.
Pity the young who want fine clothes.[36]

In the saga Cynddylan had apparently made a desperate attempt to stop the Mercians flooding across the Tren into eastern Powys. There is an exhortation to him:

Cynddylan, block the hill
Where the English come today.
It's not right to worry about one man.

Cynddylan, close up the place
Where the English come through the Tren.
'Wood' is not the word where there's one tree.[37]

But Cynddylan is overwhelmed and the eagle of Eli [38]and the eagle of Pengwern feast on the bodies of the slain:

The eagle of Eli calls strongly tonight ,
He's quaffed a bloody drink,
The heart-blood of Cynddylan Wyn.

The eagle of Pengwern has a grey crest tonight,
His screech is piercing,
Greedy for the flesh I loved.

The eagle of Pengwern has a grey crest tonight,
His cry is piercing.
Greedy for Cynddylan's flesh.[39]

Even Eglwysau Basa, the place where the hero might have expected a safe and honourable burial, is a smouldering ruin that has forfeited its ecclesiastical privileges.

Y Dref Wen, another community mentioned in the poems, may possibly be Whittington near Oswestry, or perhaps an unidentified place in Shropshire nearer the old border on the Tren.[40] Although its name might suggest a fair or holy place, the reality is that it has long been the scene of conflict and destruction:

> The white town amidst the trees
> Has always been like this:
> Blood smeared across its grass.
>
> The white town is used in its surroundings
> To grey graves,
> And blood beneath men's feet.
>
> The white town in the valley,
> Unfeelingly happy in the noise of battle,
> Its people have perished.[41]

The Heledd saga is almost unbearably bleak. Sir Ifor Williams describes it as having been produced in 'a period of acute depression, gloom and despair.'[42] The years since the historical Cynddylan had perished, probably in a fight over cattle near the border, had been difficult for the people of Powys. Eastern Powys had been lost in the years after Cynddylan's death. Offa's Dyke had then appeared like a Berlin Wall to separate the eastern cantrefi from the west forever and to ensure that Pengwern Powys would be assimilated into Mercia.

The anonymous storyteller who shaped the saga was acutely aware of the pain and *hiraeth* (that deep and agonising sense of loss for something infinitely precious that can never be restored) that the westward shift of the frontier had caused for his people. It is possible that he attempted to dramatise the anguish through his portrayal of the relationship between Heledd and her dead brother. There is a sense in which Heledd could come to represent western Powys and there are references in the poetry to places in the heartland of Caereinion from which the Cyndrwynyn had come. The dead Cynddylan might be seen as representing eastern Powys, ravaged, torn apart and lost forever.

Behind the story is a moral judgement about the fatal weakness that had somehow resulted in the loss of so much that was beautiful and precious to the people of Powys. That weakness was arrogance and pride. Perhaps in his condemnation of Heledd, the poet was remembering the days when Powys and Mercia had been allies against the Northumbrians, and was regretting that that alliance had not been maintained, but instead had turned into bitter enmity. He may however have been making a more general but even more important point: pride and arrogance destroy people and countries. It must have been a bitter lesson for his audience to listen to and learn from.

In Glyn Jones and T. J. Morgan's attempt to reconstruct the Heledd saga, the bereaved princess goes first to western Powys, the land of her ancestors, where she tends animals, becoming wilder and stranger and more deranged. In the end she finds herself drawn back across the new border to the hilltops of the area once ruled by her brother: to the Ercall and the ancient hill-fort of the Wrekin. She looks down from the Wrekin across the land where her brothers fought and died and then she lies down and her own life comes to an end. Her heart has been broken by a combination of sorrow at the losses she has suffered and remorse at the tragedy for which she feels responsible.[43]

NOTES

[1] Negative attitudes towards the marriage of saints are a common feature in Welsh hagiography. See the examples cited by Elissa Henken, *The Welsh Saints: A Study in Patterned Lives* (Cambridge, 1991), p.175. Presumably the hagiographers were attempting to promote the image of the celibate cleric. Throughout the Middle Ages church authorities in Wales had problems imposing celibacy on their priests. Williams, *Welsh Church*, pp.16, 41, 339-46.

[2] Bartrum, *Welsh Classical Dictionary*, pp.585-6 ('Selyf Sarffgadau ap Cynan Garwyn').

[3] *The Elucidarium and other tracts in Welsh from Llyvr Agkyr Llandewivrevi*, editd by J. Morris Jones and John Rhys (Oxford, 1894), pp.119-27. See also the edition of the life in *Vitae Sanctorum Britanniae et Genealogiae*, edited by A.W. Wade-Evans (Cardiff, 1944), pp.16-22. There is a recent English translation in Oliver Davies and Thomas O'Loughlin, *Celtic Spirituality* (New York and Mahwah, 1999), pp.213-20.

[4] Baring-Gould and Fisher, *Lives*, I, 210. *Gwaith Y Parch. Walter Davies, A.C. (Gwallter Mechain)*, edited by D. Silvan Evans, 3 vols (Carmarthen, 1868), III, 1.

[5] Baring-Gould and Fisher, *Lives*, I, 210, point out the presence of 'Tredderwen' ('the township of the oak') in Llanymynech parish as an additional item of evidence

supporting the idea that it was Beuno's birthplace and the place where his father was buried. Another possibility might be that a peculiarly shaped oak tree in this border community gave rise to the story, which was then attached to the life of Beuno. Onomastic legends are fascinating folklore but rarely possess historical value.

[6] Bartrum, *Welsh Classical Dictionary*, p.460 ('Mawn ap Brochwel Ysgithrog'). Baring-Gould and Fisher, *Lives*, I, 211, claim that the life is incorrect and that Mawn was Brochwel's brother.

[7] Thomas, *History*, III,128-9. The tradition connecting the stone with Beuno may, of course, be comparatively recent.

[8] Bartrum, *Welsh Classical Dictionary*, p.627 ('Tyfid ab Eiludd').

[9] Medieval versions of the life of Gwenfrewi are listed in Cartrwight, *Y Forwyn Fair, Santesau a Lleianod*, pp.83-4.

[10] The anchorite of Llanddewibrefi may possibly have used a no longer extant Latin life of Beuno as his source.

[11] Elissa R. Henken, *Traditions of the Welsh Saints* (Cambridge, 1987), pp.74-80. Perhaps the most famous example is in the fifteenth-century poet Lewys Glyn Cothi's heart-rending elegy for his little son, Siôn y Glyn, where he wishes that Siôn might be the eighth person brought back to life by Beuno. See *Galar y Beirdd: Marwnadau Plant / Poets' Grief: Medieval Welsh Elegies for Children*, edited and translated by Dafydd Johnston (Cardiff, 1993), pp.102-3.

[12] Nennius, *British History and The Welsh Annals,* edited and translated by John Morris (London, 1980), pp. 46, 86; Bede, *A History of the English Church and People* (Harmondsworth, 1965), pp.101-2. The date given for the battle of Chester in the *Annales Cambriae* is 613.

[13] *Trioedd Ynys Prydein*, edited by Rachel Bromwich (Cardiff, 1961), pp.163-5; 389-91, 436.

[14] The fourth of the *'Englynion Cadwallon'*. See Rowland, *Early Welsh Saga Poetry*, pp.446, 495.

[15] Bromwich, *Trioedd,* 182-3; 295.

[16] N.J. Higham, *The Kingdom of Northumbria AD 350-1100* (Stroud, 1993), p.129.

[17] Williams, *Canu Llywarch Hen,* pp.48, 242; *Gwaith Cynddelw Brydydd Mawr,* I, 31, 45; Rowland, *Early Welsh Saga Poetry,* pp.124-5.

[18] Wendy Davies, *Wales in the Early Middle Ages* (Leicester, 1982), pp.99-102; White and Barker, *Wroxeter,* p.132.

[19] Gerald of Wales, *The Journey through Wales/The Description of Wales* (Harmondsworth, 1978), p.139.

[20] Williams, *Canu Llywarch Hen,* pp.192-3; John Davies, *Hanes Cymru* (London, 1990), p.63; White and Barker, *Wroxeter,* p.132.

[21] For the earlier poem see Williams, *Canu Llywarch Hen,* pp.50-2; R. Geraint Gruffydd, *'Marwnad Cynddylan'* in *Bardos: Penodau ar y Traddodiad Barddol Cymreig a Cheltaidd,* edited by R. Geraint Gruffydd (Cardiff, 1982), pp.10-28; also Rowland, *Early Welsh Saga Poetry,* 174-89. For the later cycle see Williams, *Canu Llywarch Hen,* pp.33-48; Rowland, *Early Welsh Saga Poetry,* pp.120-69; 429-45; 483-94.

[22] Gruffydd,'*Marwnad Cynddylan'*, p.23.

[23] Gruffydd, '*Marwnad Cynddylan*,' pp.25-6.

[24] Rowland, *Early Welsh Saga Poetry*, pp.133-5.

[25] Rowland, *Early Welsh Saga Poetry*, p.189.

[26] Davies, *Wales in the Early Middle Ages,* p.100.

[27] Williams, *Canu Llywarch Hen* , pp.35-37. In translating this poem and some of the other verses from the Heledd saga, as well as the poetry of the historical Taliesin, I have referred to the modernized Welsh versions contained in *Yr Aelwyd Hon*, edited by Gwyn Thomas (Llandybie, 1970). For a recent scholarly translation of the Heledd poems see Rowland, *Early Welsh Saga Poetry*, pp.483-94.

[28] Gerald, *Journey,* p.223.

[29] *Brut,* p.4.

[30] Glyn Jones and T. J. Morgan, *The Story of Heledd*, edited by Jenny Rowland (Newtown, 1994).

[31] Perhaps the mead-swilling warriors of Aneirin's *Gododdin* influenced the two authors in their reconstruction. See Ifor Williams, *Canu Aneirin* (Cardiff, 1970).

[32] Williams, *Canu Llywarch Hen*, p.42.

[33] Williams, *Canu Llywarch Hen*, p.40.

[34] Williams, *Canu Llywarch Hen*, p.39.

[35] Williams, *Canu Llywarch Hen*, p.44.

[36] Williams, *Canu Llywarch Hen*, p.33.

[37] Williams, *Canu Llywarch Hen*, p.35.

[38] Meheli in Montgomeryshire, not far from the original home of the Cyndrwynyn, Heledd's family.

[39] Williams, *Canu Llywarch Hen*, p.38.

[40] Williams, *Canu Llywarch Hen*, pp.215-16.

[41] Williams, *Canu Llywarch Hen*, pp.39-40.

[42] Williams, *Beginnings of Welsh Poetry*, pp.150-1. In *Y Traddodiad Barddol* (Cardiff, 1976), p.81, Gwyn Thomas challenged this idea. He comments about the Llywarch Hen and Heledd material: 'I find it difficult to see a storytelling poet creating situations for two old characters from the past in order to portray the present that existed in Powys in 850: that would involve too much intentional composition for an oral period.' Jenny Rowland produces a persuasive solution to the problem in *Early Welsh Saga Poetry*, pp.140-1.

[43] The ending of the 'reconstruction' is clearly derived from the death of Branwen. See Williams, *Pedeir Keinc y Mabinogi*, p.45.

3. GWRNERTH AND LLYWELYN

i) Cynddylan's Saintly Nephews

According to a medieval Welsh genealogy, the Cyndrwynyn produced saints as well as warriors and princesses. Cynddylan had a brother called Cerfael ap Cyndrwyn. Cerfael's three sons, Aelhaearn, Cynhaearn and Llwchaearn, were all regarded as founders of churches. Aelhaearn is the patron of three churches: Guilsfield (Cegidfa), just north of Welshpool, a Llanaelhaearn which came under Gwyddelwern in Edeirnion and a second Llanaelhaearn which came under Clynnog in Arfon. This second Llanelhaearn and its nearby holy well dedicated to the saint became stopping places for medieval pilgrims on their way to Ynys Enlli (Bardsey).[1]

All three churches are in areas connected with Beuno. Guilsfield is in the border district of Powys from which Beuno originally came. It is also not far from Meifod, where the saint fled after his encounter with the Englishman mentioned above. Gwyddelwern was said to have been named after an Irishman whom Beuno brought back from the dead. It was also the place where he quarrelled with Cynan Garwyn's sons before moving on to settle near Gwenfrewi's parents. Clynnog Fawr was the great monastic centre established by Beuno in Arfon and the place where his wanderings finally came to an end. The claim that Aelhaearn was one of Beuno's disciples is therefore a convincing one. The link between the two saints is strengthened by the inclusion, in four sixteenth-century lists, of Aelhaearn as one of the six people whom Beuno is said to have brought back to life.[2]

This tradition is also mentioned in a poem by Lewis Môn (fl. c. 1480-1527). He refers to Aelhaearn being broken in two, with his bones scattered apart and wolves tearing his flesh.[3] The background to the poet's remarks is provided by a rather startling folk story that was collected by the seventeenth-century naturalist John Ray. The legend said that Aelhaearn was Beuno's inquisitive servant. Every night the holy man used to walk the four miles from Clynnog Fawr to what is now

Llanaelhaearn. There he would pray on a stone in the river. Local people still showed the stone to curious visitors. They claimed that the grooves in it were marks left by the saint's knees as he knelt in prayer. The servant wanted to know why his master disappeared every night. He followed Beuno to the river and watched him.

When the saint finished his prayers, he noticed that someone was spying on him. So he prayed that if the stranger's intentions were good he might receive the thing that he had come for and be unharmed. But Beuno also prayed that if the person intended any evil he should be taught a lesson. Which he was – in a peculiarly savage way. Wild beasts suddenly appeared and tore the snooper to bits. Beuno then noticed that the victim was his own servant and felt sorry for him. He carefully gathered all the bits together and prayed over them, and the man was restored to life. Unfortunately a bone under the servant's eyebrow was still missing. Beuno used the iron tip of his staff to make up the deficiency and from then onwards the servant was known as Aelhaearn ('iron brow').[4]

While the story certainly echoes the other traditions that were mentioned earlier about Beuno's appallingly effective curses and his equally effective gift for restoring the dead to life, one can sympathise with the traveller, Thomas Pennant, who dismissed it as 'a legend too absurd to relate.'[5] The tale was nothing more than an imaginative attempt to explain Aelhaearn's peculiar name. Cynhaearn, another of the three brothers, also apparently travelled to Gwynedd (presumably with Beuno). He is commemorated in the place name of Ynyscynhaearn in Eifionydd, but no traditions or stories about him seem to have survived.[6]

Baring-Gould and Fisher mention a medieval Welsh calendar that stresses Aelhaern's Montgomeryshire connections, referring to him as being 'of Cegidfa in Powys.' The English name for Cegidfa is Guilsfield. They also record that 'at Guilsfield, a mile and a half from the Church, is a Holy Well, in a lovely secluded dell, where still a concourse gathers to drink the water on Trinity Sunday.'[7] D. R. Thomas refers to a *'Fons Tysilio'* in Guilsfield, mentioned as a boundary landmark in the founding charter of the abbey of Ystrad Marchell. Guilsfield church is dedicated to both Aelhaearn and Tysilio. This may perhaps indicate that Aelhaearn began as a disciple of Tysilio's and then left to join Beuno on his travels – or it may be a sign that the Meifod community took over a church originally founded by Aelhaearn.[8]

The third brother, Llwchaearn, stayed in mid-Wales. At some point he must have wandered over to Ceredigion as there are two churches dedicated to him there: Llanllwchaearn (Newquay) on the shores of Cardigan Bay and Llanychaearn just outside Aberystwyth. However the centre of his cult (and therefore presumably of his life and ministry) was Llanllwchaearn (or Llanllwchaiarn) and Llanmerewig (originally Llamyrewig), two parishes east of Y Drenewydd (Newtown) in southeast Montgomeryshire. Both are in the rural deanery of Cedewain, as is Ceri (Kerry), which was the home of the prolific poet Siôn ap y Bedo ap Deio Fychan (Siôn Ceri) in the first half of the sixteenth century. It is thanks to Siôn Ceri that we know something of the local traditions about Llwchaearn. One of Siôn's patrons was Rhys ap Morys ab Owain ab Ieuan Blaenau of Aberbechan in the parish of Llanllwchaearn. The poet composed a *cywydd* in honour of Llwchaearn, asking him to bless Rhys.[9]

Siôn Ceri's poem in praise of the saint calls him the son of Cynfael. Elsewhere he is described as the son of Caranfael ap Cyndrwyn.[10] Caranfael is the name of Cynddylan's son in the Heledd saga (though the earlier lament to Cynddylan makes it clear that he did not have any children).[11] The most reliable genealogical tradition records Llwchaearn as one of Cerfael ap Cyndrwyn's sons, which suggests that mistakes by copyists are doubtless responsible for the confusion.[12] The poet also claims that the saint was Beuno's cousin. This idea may stem from the close connection between Beuno and Aelhaearn. Apart from a few fragmentary folk traditions, Siôn Ceri probably had very little raw material for his poem, but he used his fertile imagination to fill in the gaps. His picture of the ascetic saint is attractive, even if he does rather improbably promote Llwchaearn to the episcopate:

> You are a man whom God made
> To lead a good path as abbot and bishop.
> You came to pray
> Below a hill on the other side of the Severn.
> There you once would hear the bell
> Ringing before its time.
> A shirt was made, you'll receive grace,
> Out of horsehair that was virtuous.
> You prayed for nine months,

> Nine nights and nine days,
> And your two knees in penance
> Were bruised on the cold grey stone.[13]

It may be that there was a stone reputed to be marked by the knees of the praying saint in the river Severn at Llanllwchaearn, like Beuno's stone in the river at Llanaelhaearn.[14]

The poet tells us that Llwchaearn was granted nine requests, presumably as a result of the 'nine months, nine nights and nine days' that he had spent in knee-bruising prayer on the cold grey stone. Three of the nine were personal. They were the salvation of the saint's soul, the ability to reject sin and the power to keep Christ's commandments. Three more were to benefit pilgrims who came to Llwchaearn's shrine and the final three were concerned with blessing the people of the parish (and their animals) in this life and assuring their souls a place in heaven in the life to come.

The tension between military and spiritual heroism is a strand that runs through the cultural history of the border area in pre-Reformation times.[15] Tysilio was said to have turned his back on princely warlike duties in order to pursue a peaceful life of prayer. However, as we have seen, Cynddelw Brydydd Mawr portrayed him as a militant saint, urging the hosts of Powys on to victory at the battle of Cogwy from his vantage point in heaven. Siôn Ceri attempts to square the circle by making Llwchaearn a soldier saint, modelled on the most famous one of Christian legend:

> You are a great saviour,
> A soldier saint like splendid George.[16]

Three creatures were apparently causing anxiety in the area: a wild boar, a serpent and a hind. Llwchaearn got rid of all three. He killed the serpent with his own hands and tricked the hind into jumping into a pit where it would stay until the Day of Judgement:

> Your men would not have had life
> Unless this hind had been made to fall.
> Your trap, son, was a brave way to do it,
> Your miracle that shortened her life.[17]

Behind this story is an attempt to explain the name of Llwchaearn's parish of Llanmerewig, which in Siôn Ceri's time was still known as Llamyrewig ('the hart's leap'), a form first found in a document of 1254.[18]

Siôn praises Llwchaearn's two churches in the valley of the river Severn, regarding them as at least as important a centre of prayer, blessing and pilgrimage as Ynys Enlli (Bardsey Island), the great pilgrimage shrine of Gwynedd:

> May God's grace always flow abundantly
> Through your lovely miracles by the Severn.
> Your miracle was the length of the blue sea
> Over there that doubled to two places.
> Two altars are even better than one good place,
> And a great offering continues.
> Your earth is a sanctuary:
> A saint is its magistrate yonder.
> Your grace is no less than that of distant Enlli.
> The weak know that a word from you can bring
> A hundred miracles, my splendid lord.
> Innocent faultless one – listen to his judgement,
> Heal the guilty, Llwchaearn.[19]

Even on the eve of the Reformation, one of Cynddylan's saintly nephews could still inspire a poet's imagination, becoming a source of hope and pride and consolation for the people of two small communities by the river Severn. Further north along the same valley, at Welshpool, two other holy men had also made a lasting impression.

ii) The Community of Trallwng Llywelyn

Llyfr Coch Hergest (The Red Book of Hergest) is one of the great manuscripts of medieval Wales. It was written by a scribe named Hywel Fychan fab Hywel Goch of Builth for his patron, Hopcyn ap Tomas ab Einion, at the end of the fourteenth century. Tucked away among its contents are two conversations, embedded in a setting of rather conventional poetic description. The first conversation is between a living and a dying man. The latter dies and yet it is he, after his death, who initiates the second discussion with the living man.[20]

On the face of it, the identity of the two who are talking seems straightforward. The verses have a short prose introduction that begins: 'Llywelyn and Gwrnerth were two penitential saints in Y Trallwng (Welshpool) in Powys.' There is also a note at the end to show that the verses, known as 'The Penance of Gwrnerth and Llywelyn,' were once in the possession of Tysilio, son of Brochwel Ysgithrog.[21] This suggests that Llywelyn and Gwrnerth were at the very least contemporaries of Tysilio and that they possibly pre-date him. Indeed the fertile imagination of Iolo Morganwg made Llywelyn the father of Gwyddfarch, presumably a reference to Tysilio's teacher at Meifod.[22] However Peter Bartrum, the authority on early Welsh genealogies, suggests that Llywelyn and Gwrnerth lived in the second half of the ninth century. This would mean that they were alive around the time that the Heledd saga was being composed.[23]

A chapel-of-ease dedicated to St Llywelyn stood on the site of his cell for many centuries, some two hundred yards to the east of St Mary's Church in Welshpool. It was destroyed in a fire on Christmas Day 1659. An undated picture of the ruins of Capel Llywelyn is included by D.J. Thomas in the illustrated edition of his *History of the Diocese of St Asaph*. He describes Llywelyn and Gwrnerth as 'the founders of a community, afterwards known as Trallwng Llywelyn, the precursor of the Abbey of Strata Marcella, whose misfortunes it shared on its dissolution.'[24]

Jenny Rowland regards the Llywelyn and Gwrnerth verses in *Llyfr Coch Hergest* as being of a type dating from the late eleventh or early twelfth centuries.[25] One of the verses from the poem has also been discovered copied carefully into a thirteenth-century manuscript that came originally from Margam Abbey. The orthography of this copy suggested to F.G. Cowley and Nesta Lloyd that it came from a poem written down by the eleventh century, and possibly before.[26] The abbey of Ystrad Marchell was not founded until 1170. This means that the likely source of the poem is the religious community of Trallwng Llywelyn. The reference to Tysilio might suggest Meifod as an alternative source, but it was probably only included in an attempt to reinforce the antiquity and authenticity of the poetry. The poem thus contains what is supposed to be a conversation between two men who lived perhaps a couple of centuries before it was written. The introduction and end-note (presumably added some time after the poem was written) were carefully framed to suggest that those men actually lived in the sixth century rather than the ninth.

A further complication is caused by the difference of the relationship between the two men in the poem and that conventionally ascribed to Llywelyn and Gwrnerth. According to the genealogies, Llywelyn was the father of Gwrnerth, who must therefore have died young. However the text in the *Llyfr Coch* says nothing about this and instead implies that the connection between the two men is a spiritual one. They are both described as 'penitential saints'. In the first section Llywelyn refers to Gwrnerth as *fy mrawt* ('my brother') and when Gwrnerth appears to Llywelyn in the second part of the poem he identifies himself with the words *'Mae yma dy vrawt, Gwrnerth'* ('Your brother Gwrnerth is here').[27]

The two men are thus portrayed in the poem as fellow members of a religious community. They would appear to be two hermits living in separate cells and meeting together before dawn every morning to spend time in prayer together. In the second half of the poem, the dead Gwrnerth gives spiritual advice to Llywelyn (with all the authority of a man whose home is now in heaven). However the type of advice is very much that which might be given by a spiritual counsellor to his disciple. This would normally mean a younger person going to an older person for direction. An example from elsewhere might be that of a would-be monk going off to see one of the 'old men' of the Egyptian desert and requesting, 'Abba, give me a word'; or perhaps a worried young layman or woman in nineteenth century Russia making a pilgrimage to Optino to seek spiritual counsel from one of the venerable startsy (spiritual elders) there.[28]

In terms of the religious history of Powys, a similar pattern is provided by the relationship between Gwyddfarch and Tysilio, as expressed in Albert Le Grand's depiction of them, though it is interesting that the roles of the two are reversed towards the end of Gwyddfarch's life. In the beginning Gwyddfarch is the young prince's guide. It is he who teaches Tysilio about the Christian faith and develops his inclination towards the religious life. Gwyddfarch admits Tysilio to the community in Meifod and arranges a safe refuge for him so that he will not be forced to return to court. Towards the end of Gwyddfarch's life however, it is Tysilio who starts to take the initiative. He tries to persuade the old abbot to abandon his passionate desire to make a pilgrimage to Rome. Tysilio's prayers secure the vision that becomes a substitute for the pilgrimage, and Tysilio's hand leads Gwyddfarch up the hillock so that they can share that vision. This suggests that, in the traditions of Powys, both an old man and a young man may, under the appropriate circumstances, become effective spiritual guides.

The daily office of prayer outlined in the introduction is probably that of the community of Trallwng Llywelyn at the time that the poem was composed. It may very well reflect the pattern of life established by the founder or founders of the community a couple of centuries before. We are told that the two 'penitential saints' used 'to come together for the last three hours of the night and the first three hours of the day to recite their pre-dawn prayers and their prayers of the day as well.' The word used for the pre-dawn prayers is *pylgeint,* which comes from the Latin *pulli cantus* ('cock-crowing').[29]

Plygain or *Pylgain* is most commonly used in modern Welsh as the name of the Welsh Christmas service that traditionally began at between three and six o'clock in the morning on Christmas Day. It was originally a Communion service (and remains so in some of the west Wales parishes in which I have served, still being held before dawn at 6 a.m.). Its origins were either the Midnight Mass or, more probably in my opinion, an early morning Mass held to commemorate the visit by the shepherds to the manger in Bethlehem (perhaps as the result of the influence of the Franciscans in Wales). In rural Montgomeryshire, *Plygain* became associated with the composition and singing of carols in the post-Reformation period. *Plygain* carols tend to have a considerable doctrinal content, linking the incarnation and the crucifixion and outlining the history of salvation. The tradition was and is especially strong in the valleys of the rivers Banw, Tanat and Vyrnwy, though *Plygain* services are no longer held specifically on Christmas Day before dawn in those areas, but instead are held on varying dates between Christmas and Epiphany, often in the evening.[30]

In early medieval Wales however, *pylgeint* was the name of a daily early morning service that usually began at about 6 a.m. Cynddelw refers to the singing of *pylgeint* by the monks of Meifod in his poem of praise to St Tysilio:

I, Cynddelw, before the time I lose my skill,
Claim patronage through privilege:
I sang a new poem to my lord
With a splendid inspiration that came with the breeze of the *pylgeint.*

I am given the honours of the *pylgeinnau,*
The blessing of generous wisdom, they are excellently sung . . .[31]

After the Reformation the word *plygain* was occasionally still used for a morning office among Welsh-speaking Anglicans. Thus when a Welsh version of the Primer or shortened Book of Common Prayer for lay use appeared in 1612, it was entitled *Y Llyfr Plygain.*[32] In the experimental service produced for the Church in Wales in 1969, *Plygain* was still given as an alternative name for *Boreol Wéddi* (Morning Prayer or Mattins). This was dropped from the 1984 definitive book.[33]

The brothers of Trallwng Llywelyn apparently divided their daily services into two categories. First they said three hours of *pylgeint* before dawn. This was followed by three more hours of prayer after dawn during which they recited *oryeu y dydd* (the daytime 'hours' or offices). It was a fairly hefty chunk of devotional exercises for anyone to undertake. We can readily sympathise with poor Llywelyn in the second part of the poem, when he dozes off in the middle of his early morning orisons. The normal pattern in most monastic communities was to divide the office up, saying parts of it at different times of the day. Gwrnerth, Llywelyn and their spiritual descendants seem to have preferred one long marathon of prayer, which then left them free to devote the rest of the day to other duties and activities.

The introduction sets the scene for the first part of the poem: 'Llywelyn saw that Gwrnerth's cell was closed and, because he did not know why that was, he sang a verse.' In the translation below I have italicised the actual conversation to distinguish it from the framework of conventional poetic phrases in which it is set:

Llywelyn: Snow on the mountain, wind around the hedge,
            As Heaven's Creator gives me strength,
            Is Gwrnerth sleeping?

Gwrnerth: Snow on the mountain, *God is supreme,*
            As I pray to him;
            No, I cannot sleep.

Llywelyn: Snow on the mountain, wind around the house,
                 As you speak in this way,
                 What, Gwrnerth, is causing that?

Gwrnerth: Snow on the mountain, wind from the south,
                 As I recite the important phrases,
                 Most probably it is death.

Llywelyn: Snow on the mountain, dazzling white all around,
                 Everyone is happy in his patron's eyes;
                 May Heaven's Creator save you.

Gwrnerth: Snow on the mountain, the tree shining white,
                 As I say differently,
                 There's no refuge from fate.

                 Snow on the mountain, *every custom*
                 Protects against the anxiety of Judgement Day;
                 Can I beg to have Communion?

Llywelyn: Snow on the mountain, wind around the house,
                 As you speak in this way,
                 Alas, my brother, is that necessary?'

Gwrnerth: *Quick-witted one, I love you,*
                 I pray to God,
                 Llywelyn, it is too late for me to have it . . .[34]

There is a possibility that the Gwrnerth and Llywelyn poems might originally have been the verse sections of a life of the two saints using the Powys saga format of poetry set in a prose narrative. The verses have a dramatic force. As the conversation develops, the saints begin to emerge as characters. Jenny Rowland has described Llywelyn as playing 'the naïve and ill-informed straight man' in the dialogue.[35] He certainly comes across as hugely well intentioned but rather slow on the uptake. Gwrnerth, on the other hand, is a realist who faces up to his impending death with courage and shows considerable patience in his attitude towards Llywelyn.

Just a hint of irony creeps in at the end of the first conversation. Gwrnerth knows that he has been deprived of the possibility of receiving the final Communion that he so desperately wanted by Llywelyn's time-wasting combination of panic and hoping for the best. At the beginning of the last verse he addresses his procrastinating friend as *awendrut* ('a person who has a ready muse' –'quick-witted one' seems an appropriate translation). The joke is underlined by the fact that this is the only verse that doesn't begin with a reference to mountain snow. However Gwrnerth immediately qualifies this gentle dig by adding '*mi a'th garaf*' ('I love you'). Living in community is always a considerable test of mutual tolerance and a demanding school in which to learn (with God's help) the difficult skill of loving our neighbour as God loves us. Living in a community of two with Llywelyn as the other half must have been a particular strain at times. Gwrnerth's sainthood was well earned – though, as he says, there is indeed something loveable about his anxious and well-meaning brother. Any monk who heard the first section of the poem being recited would immediately be able to identify the Gwrnerths and the Llywelyns in his community (and hopefully might well see something of himself in one or both of the characters as well).

The opening conversation takes place against a conventional backdrop of snow on the mountain and wind whistling around hedges and houses. The coldness of winter provides an appropriate context for Gwrnerth's death. The Welsh idiom for a bitter east wind, *gwynt traed y meirw*, comes to mind, and we can easily visualise the snow on the hills around Welshpool.[36] However the use of the opening words '*Eiry mynydd*' ('Snow on the mountain') at the beginning of each verse would have had a special resonance for the poem's original audience. '*Eiry mynydd*' is one of the characteristic phrases used in early Welsh gnomic poems: a series of didactic verses used to convey proverbial wisdom. For example one such verse which would have immediately come to mind when the poem began (and which might have inspired the Gwrnerth and Llywelyn poet to use this form) is

> Snow on the mountain, white all around.
> A crow is used to singing.
> No good comes from oversleeping.[37]

The monks, hermits or 'penitential saints' of the community of Trallwng Llywelyn seem to have lived in separate huts or cells within an enclosure with a small church or chapel (perhaps the original Capel Llywelyn) at its centre, where they would gather to say their prayers. Leaving their cells three hours before dawn must have been a severe trial sometimes.

No doubt as he hammered on the door of some particularly somnolent brother, their superior would be tempted to repeat the poet's proverb: 'No good comes from oversleeping'.

iii) A Pattern of Life

Gwrnerth died and for a time at any rate, if the poet is to be believed, the fledgling community of Trallwng Llywelyn was reduced to a single hermit. Praying on your own in a cold church in the hours before dawn can be a desolating experience at times. Llywelyn was cold and lonely and extremely tired. As he tried to go through the prayers of the *pylgeint*, his eyelids drooped and his mind wandered and he began to doze. He was startled back into wakefulness by an unexpected voice. Once again I have put the actual conversation into italics.

Gwrnerth: Snow on the mountain, wind around the hill,
As Heaven's Creator, wants me to ask,
Is Llywelyn sleeping?

Llywelyn: Snow on the mountain, wind from the south,
As I recite the important phrases,
No, I am singing my office.

Gwrnerth: Snow on the mountain, *learned man,*
When the wind turns around the wall,
Do you know who's speaking?

Llywelyn: Snow on the mountain, *bold talker,*
Since you mention it,
I don't, unless you tell me.

Gwrnerth: Snow on the mountain, every help
Will be beautifully praised;
Your brother Gwrnerth is here.

Llywelyn: The disturbance of a great poem, and the energy of every eager man,
And the muse impelling me:
What, Gwrnerth, is best in your opinion?

Gwrnerth: The prominence of every ritual and the striving nature of an eager man;

Concerning life till Judgement Day,
I have found almsgiving to be best.

Llywelyn: *Quick-witted one, with so many fair achievements,*
The rule is on your lips:
Say what kind of almsgiving is best.

Gwrnerth: Daring poet, the wind is by the lake
When a wave drives itself around the hill;
The best thing is food against hunger.

Llywelyn: *If I cannot find food,*
Or get it with my hands,
Say what I should do then.

Gwrnerth: The disturbance of a great poem, and the energy of every
eager man,
And the muse impelling me:
Give clothes against nakedness.

Llywelyn: *I shall give my clothes,*
Bequeathing them to God,
What reward shall I have then?

Gwrnerth: *Whatever goods you give in true penitence,*
Eagerly as if to preserve your honour,
Shall be given to you in Heaven a hundred-fold.

Llywelyn: Day-coloured one, as I love you,
Author of poems, as I seek you,
What does God hate most?

Gwrnerth: Profit and poetry and company,
When the water runs downwards,
The worst thing is deception through betrayal of trust.

Llywelyn: *If I deceive through betrayal of trust,*
And if I don't confess that to God,
What vengeance shall I suffer?

Gwrnerth: *If you deceive through betrayal of trust,*
Without faith, without religion, without belief,
You shall have a sevenfold penance.

Llywelyn:	Daylight-coloured one, *I believe you,*
	And for God's sake I ask you:
	How may I reach Heaven?
Gwrnerth:	Good and bad are not alike,
	When wind and smoke fight together,
	Do good for God's sake, that is pay him his due.
Llywelyn:	Leading friend of the muse of every refuge,
	Horses are great runners in warm weather,
	Confession is the end of everything.
Gwrnerth:	*Whatever sin you may commit,*
	Deceit, violence or pride,
	For God's sake, confess well.[38]

This second section begins with some banter that reflects the character of the two saints that had already been established in the first part. Gwrnerth's ghost is able to get his own back on Llywelyn by aiming the latter's original question back at him: 'Is Llywelyn sleeping?' He then goes on to tease the drowsy hermit by trying to get him to guess who is speaking to him. Once Gwrnerth has revealed his identity, Llywelyn feels free to ask his advice. Gwrnerth is dead and therefore is in a position to look back on his earthly existence and counsel his former companion about what is truly important in human existence.

His suggestions are straightforward. Llywelyn should practise charity of the most basic and uncomplicated kind. He should feed the hungry and, if his resources do not permit him to do so, he should clothe the naked. Llywelyn's response to this advice gives the impression that the hermits of Trallwng Llywelyn led a very austere existence. Food seems to have been in short supply, but Llywelyn was quite happy to give the shirt (or habit) off his own back if that would help someone in need. Giraldus Cambrensis, writing perhaps a hundred years after the composition of the Llywelyn and Gwrnerth poem, praises Welsh anchorites for their abstinence and spiritual commitment, which he ascribes to a Welsh tendency to go to extremes in everything. His remarks may well have been based on what he heard about the communities of hermits on Ynys Enlli (Bardsey) and Ynys Lannog (Priestholm) while travelling around Wales with Archbishop Baldwin. However there is no reason to think that they might not have applied just as well to the community of Trallwng Llywelyn.[39]

The charitable actions recommended by Gwrnerth have their origins in Jesus' injunctions in the Gospel. 'If you wish to be perfect, go, sell your possessions and give to the poor, and you will have treasure in heaven; then come and follow me.' (Matthew 19.21). 'When I was hungry, you gave me food; when thirsty, you gave me drink; when I was a stranger, you took me into your home; when naked, you clothed me; when I was ill, you came to my help; when in prison, you visited me . . . anything you did for one of my brothers here, however insignificant, you did for me.' (Matthew 25.35-6, 40). A straightforward acceptance of these principles had been the most powerful impetus to the development of Christian monasticism, initially in the Egyptian desert.

As well as wanting to know what he should do, Llywelyn is also anxious to find out what he should avoid.

The answer again is a stark and simple one. The greatest sin, the thing that God hates most, Gwrnerth tells his friend, is *'twyll trwy ymdiret'* – deceit that stems from a betrayal of trust. That is the sort of betrayal which Adam and Eve were guilty of in the Garden of Eden and which Judas Iscariot committed when he handed Jesus over to his enemies with a treacherous kiss in the Garden of Gethsemane. Mutual trust plays a central part in the life of any community. If the members of the community of Trallwng Llywelyn could base their lives on it, their example might have an impact on the wider world.

If Jenny Rowland's assumption that the Gwrnerth and Llywelyn verses were written in the late eleventh or early twelfth century is accepted, that message about trust and betrayal would have had a very deep resonance with their audience. Two rulers had won the admiration of the people of Powys during that period. The first was Gruffudd ap Llywelyn ap Seisyll, who had become ruler of Gwynedd and Powys in 1039.[40] He immediately made a name for himself by winning a crushing victory over the Mercians at Rhyd-y-groes-ar-Hafren, the ford across the river Severn to the east of Welshpool. This was a spot which a ninth or tenth-century writer had already linked with Cadwallon's early seventh-century sevenfold battle of Gwaith Digoll, in which he was said to have defeated Edwin of Northumbria.[41] It would also be the scene of the conflict in *Breuddwyd Rhonabwy*, which will be discussed later.[42]

This important victory so near to Trallwng Llywelyn at what was already a historic place must have made a lasting impression on the brethren of the community. It would no doubt have led them to share the horror felt by the chronicler of the *Brut* when he described Gruffudd's ultimate fate: 'One thousand and sixty-one was the year of Christ when Gruffudd ap Llywelyn was slain, after innumerable victories and taking of spoils and treasures of gold and silver and precious purple raiment, through the treachery of his own men, after his fame and glory had increased and after he had aforetimes been unconquered, but was now left in the waste valleys, and after he had been head and shield and defender of the Britons.'[43]

Gruffudd ap Llywelyn, who had added Deheubarth to Gwynedd and Powys, and thus become virtual ruler of Wales, had fallen victim to *twyll trwy ymdiret*. The same was the fate of the second great hero of the period. Bleddyn ap Cynfyn had joined his brother Rhiwallon in ruling the lands of Gruffudd, their half-brother, after the latter's death. R.R. Davies describes them as 'puppet rulers . . . installed by Edward the Confessor on his own terms.'[44] In 1067-8 the two brothers assisted the Mercian resistance against the Norman invasion.[45] Then in 1069 Ithel and Maredudd, two of Gruffudd's sons, rebelled. At the battle of Mechain both Rhiwallon and Gruffudd's sons were killed. Bleddyn emerged as the sole ruler of Gwynedd and Powys.[46] From then onwards he had to fight off Norman incursions. However it was not the Normans who killed him, but a fellow Welshman.

The *Brut* records that in 1075 'Bleddyn ap Cynfyn was slain through the evil-spirited treachery of the princes and leading men of Ystrad Tywi, he who eminently held the kingdom of all the Britons after Gruffudd, his brother. And it was Rhys ab Owain who slew him.'[47] Three years later Trahaearn ap Caradog, king of Gwynedd and a cousin of Bleddyn's, invaded Deheubarth and defeated Rhys ab Owain at the battle of Pwllgwdig. The chronicler uses this victory to express his admiration of Bleddyn, whose blood had now been avenged, saying that he 'was the most beloved and the most merciful of all kings and who wrought good to all and did harm to no one. He was gentle towards his kinsmen and generous towards the poor and merciful towards pilgrims and orphans and widows. And he was a defence for the weak and the strength of the learned and the honour of the churches, and the foundation and comfort of the lands and generous towards all; terrible in war, beloved and meek in peace and a defence for all.'[48]

Despite all these virtues, Bleddyn too had been killed as the result of *twyll trwy ymdiret*. After Pwllgwdig the army of his murderers fell apart. For a time Rhys ab Owain was on the run 'like a wounded frightened stag through the thorns and the briars before the hounds', as the chronicler records with grim satisfaction.[49] Before the year was out the fugitive was dead, killed by a rival claimant to the throne of Deheubarth. Bleddyn ap Cynfyn's descendants became the ruling dynasty in Powys. His grandson was Madog ap Maredudd, who died in 1160 and was buried in the church at Meifod. He would be the last king of a united Powys.[50]

Twyll trwy ymdiret was thus a very live issue in the political life of Powys in the late eleventh century as well as being important in the spiritual and community life of Trallwng Llywelyn. Gwrnerth describes those who are guilty of it as being 'without faith, without religion, without belief.' It is a complete negation of the Christian life and the penance for such behaviour will inevitably be very harsh. Nevertheless the fact that penance is possible provides a way in which the wounds inflicted by treacherous deception may begin to be healed. That is why Llywelyn remarks that 'confession is the end of everything.'

Gwrnerth's closing exhortation to his friend is to 'confess well'. The three sins that he stresses are those which had caused particular problems in the borderland of Powys over the centuries. Deception was, as we have seen, the cause of a major crisis at a period close to the time that the poem was written. Violence had been a bone of spiritual contention ever since (if the tradition can be trusted) Tysilio turned his back on the princely succession with its demand that he become a warrior hero, and chose instead a life of peace with Gwyddfarch and the monks of Meifod. The saga poetry had emphasised that pride, the third sin, had been Heledd's weakness. It was therefore regarded as being responsible for the disaster through which Powys Pengwern had been overrun by the Mercians and lost forever.

The members of the eleventh-century community of Trallwng Llywelyn, who imagined this conversation between its founders a couple of centuries before, had not cut themselves off from the society that surrounded them. Their life was based on a solid foundation of daily prayer: six hours in church together each day with dawn as the centre point. On this foundation they built up a life governed by practical charity towards those who were in need. They fed the hungry and clothed the naked. They also attempted to develop the idea of mutual trust as the essential quality that was needed for a healthy society. Trustworthiness and truthfulness were the key: a willingness to trust others and a refusal to deceive or betray those who put their trust in them.

It was an ambitious programme, particularly given the political problems and tensions facing the borderland at the time. As a community of penitents, the brethren were well aware of the flaws of human nature. They knew that those who tried to follow the path that they set out would often stumble or fall. That was why they stressed the importance of honest and sincere repentance and confession. They saw it as providing a way out of the moral morass into which they and the people around them were often tempted to stray.

NOTES

[1] Bartrum, *Welsh Classical Dictionary*, pp.4 ('Aelhaearn ap Cerfael'), 126 ('Cerfael ap Cyndrwyn'), 172-3 ('Cyndrwyn, prince of Powys'), 419 ('Llwchaearn ap Cerfael').

[2] Bartrum, *Welsh Classical Dictionary*, pp.43-4 ('St. Beuno').

[3] *Gwaith Lewys Môn*, edited by Eurys I. Rowlands (Cardiff, 1975), p.7.

[4] Baring-Gould and Fisher, *Lives*, I, 111.

[5] Pennant, *Tours*, II, 384.

[6] Bartrum, *Welsh Classical Dictionary*, p.179 ('Cynhaearn ap Cerfael'); Baring-Gould and Fisher, *Lives*, II, 256.

[7] Baring-Gould and Fisher, *Lives*, I, 112. The calendar is in MS BL Cotton Vespasian Axiv.

[8] Thomas, *History*, III, 147.

[9] *Gwaith Siôn Ceri*, edited by A. Cynfael Lake (Aberystwyth, 1996), pp.153-5. My translation is based on this text.

[10] Baring-Gould and Fisher, *Lives*, III, 381.

[11] Williams, *Canu Llywarch Hen*, pp.45-6; Rowland, *Early Welsh Saga Poetry*, p.126.

[12] Bartrum, *Welsh Classical Dictionary*, pp.126 ('Cerfael ap Cyndrwyn'), 419 ('Llwchaearn ap Cerfael').

[13] *Gwaith Siôn Ceri*, p.153.

[14] Such stones are a staple of Welsh folklore. Baring-Gould and Fisher, *Lives*, II, 276, record that Cynwyl was supposed to have knelt in prayer in the river Annell: 'hollows are

shown in the rock, worn by the swirl of the stream, but supposed to have been indented by his knees.'

[15] Expressions of the same tension also occur elsewhere in Wales. For the traditions concerning Illtud as a soldier turned saint see Patrick Thomas, *Illtud and his World* (Llantwit Major, 2000), pp.13-15. Dafydd Nanmor describes the way in which Pedrog Paladrddellt was said to have given arms after the internecine slaughter of Camlan, ending his days as a hermit at Ferwig in Ceredigion, *The Poetical Works of Dafydd Nanmor*, edited by Thomas Roberts and Ifor Williams (Cardiff, 1923), p.15.

[16] *Gwaith Siôn Ceri*, p.154.

[17] *Gwaith Siôn Ceri*, p.154.

[18] Thomas, *History*, I, 533-4.

[19] *Gwaith Siôn Ceri*, p.154.

[20] Haycock, *Blodeugerdd,* pp.338-48.

[21] Haycock, *Blodeugerdd*, pp.340, 346.

[22] Baring-Gould and Fisher, *Lives*, III, 388.

[23] Bartrum, *Welsh Classical Dictionary*, pp.337 ('Gwrnerth ap Llywelyn'),425 ('Llywelyn o'r Trallwng').

[24] Thomas, *History*, III, 173-4.

[25] Rowland, *Early Welsh Saga Poetry*, p.389.

[26] Haycock, *Blodeugerdd*, pp.339-40.

[27] Haycock, *Blodeugerdd*, pp.342-3.

[28] For spiritual counsel in the Egyptian desert see Graham Gould, *The Desert Fathers on Monastic Community* (Oxford, 1993) and Benedicta Ward, *The Sayings of the Desert Fathers: The Alphabetical Collection* (London, 1975). John B. Dunlop, *Staretz Amvrosy* (London, 1972) is a biography of one of the most noted startsy of Optino.

[29] Haycock, *Blodeugerdd,* p.340.

[30] See *Keep the Feast: An Introduction to Plygain*, edited by Enid R. Morgan (Penarth, 2000).

[31] *Gwaith Cynddelw Brydydd Hir*, I, 30.

[32] John Ballinger and John Fisher, *Y Llyfr Plygain 1612* (Cardiff, 1931).

[33] *Yr Eglwys yng Nghymru: Gwasanaethau'r Bore a'r Hwyr* (Cowbridge, 1969), p.[5]; *Y Llyfr Gweddi Gyffredin i'w arfer yn Yr Eglwys yng Nghymru: Trefn y Foreol a'r Hwyrol Weddi* (Penarth, 1984), p.391.

[34] Haycock, *Blodeugerdd*, pp.341-2.

[35] Rowland, *Early Welsh Saga Poetry,* p.284.

[36] *Gwynt traed y meirw* literally means 'the wind of dead men's feet'. It is still the usual custom in Wales to bury the dead with their feet pointing towards the east.

[37] Jackson, *Early Welsh Gnomic Poems* (Cardiff, 1973), p.22.

[38] Haycock, *Blodeugerdd*, pp.342-6. I have translated the section in its entirety because it offers a remarkable insight into spiritual counselling in the period when the poem was written, as well as reflecting what I assume to be the spiritual ideals of the community of Trallwng Llywelyn at that time.

[39] Gerald, *Journey*, p.254.

[40] *Brut*, p.13.

[41] Rowland, *Early Welsh Saga Poetry*, pp.446, 495, 614.
[42] Melville Richards, *Breudwyt Ronabwy* (Cardiff, 1948), pp.37-8.
[43] *Brut*, p.15.
[44] R.R. Davies, *The Age of Conquest: Wales 1063-1415* (Oxford, 1991), p.24.
[45] *The Dictionary of Welsh Biography down to 1940* (London, 1959), p.40 ('Bleddyn ap Cynfyn').
[46] *Brut*, pp.15-16.
[47] *Brut*, p.16.
[48] *Brut*, p.17.
[49] *Brut*, p.17.
[50] *Dictionary of Welsh Biography*, p.608 ('Madog ap Maredudd').

4. OWAIN CYFEILIOG AND CYNDDELW BRYDYDD MAWR

i) At the Court of Madog ap Maredudd

Despite the hopes and prayers of the brothers of the community of Trallwng Llywelyn, treachery, deceit, betrayal and violence did not decrease after the death of Bleddyn ap Cynfyn. If anything, things became worse than before as his children and grandchildren jostled for power in a divided Powys. The entries in the *Brut* provide a depressing picture of internecine warfare in which family rivalries and jealousies were often aided and abetted by the machinations of the English king.

One of the lowest points came in 1111 when Bleddyn's son Iorwerth, appointed by Henry I as ruler of Powys, was brutally killed as the result of an ambush set up by his nephew, Madog ap Rhiryd. Madog had made a secret alliance with Llywarch, one of the four sons of Trahaearn ap Caradog, the king of Gwynedd who had been killed at the battle of Mynydd Carn thirty years before. Iorwerth was in a house in Caereinion. Madog and some of Llywarch's men surrounded it at night. They shouted out to say that they were there and Iorwerth and his followers began to defend themselves. Then Madog set the house on fire. Iorwerth's men fought their way out through the flames, leaving their leader in the burning building. The house began to collapse and Iorwerth made a last desperate attempt to escape. As the burning man staggered out, he was immediately stabbed to death by the spears of Madog's companions.[1]

Henry then gave Powys to Cadwgan ap Bleddyn, Iorwerth's brother. Madog and his men went to hide in the woods, waiting for the chance to dispose of the new ruler. Cadwgan decided to set up his headquarters at Trallwng Llywelyn (Welshpool), knowing that Madog was nearby. It was an unwise decision. Madog attacked him and Cadwgan, who still seems to have thought the best of his nephew, couldn't make up his mind whether to fight or run away. His men deserted him and he was captured and killed. Madog then sent messengers to the Bishop of London, who was Henry's deputy in Shrewsbury, asking for the right to rule part of Powys. The bishop, with a certain vice-regal weariness, allowed his claim, as the chronicler puts it 'not out of love for him, but out of love for the land, for he knew that they were all killing one another.' Maredudd ap Bleddyn and Owain ap Cadwgan ap Bleddyn also received power over areas of Powys.[2]

Then suddenly Madog ap Rhiryd got his comeuppance. Maredudd ap Bleddyn's war-band were crossing through Madog's territory when they came across a man out on his own. They caught him and tortured him and eventually he told them where the local warlord was spending the night. Having safely tied up their unfortunate informant, they sent out spies and set up an ambush. On the following morning they captured Madog ap Rhiryd and took him in chains to his uncle Maredudd. Maredudd then sent a message to another nephew, Owain ap Cadwgan, whose father had been one of Madog's victims. When Owain arrived, Maredudd ap Bleddyn handed the prisoner over. The chronicler records that Owain 'took [Madog ap Rhiryd] joyfully and gouged his eyes out of his head and let him go thus,' dividing his territory with his uncle.[3]

Owain ap Cadwgan was also to suffer as the result of a past action. Several years before, he had raped and abducted Nest, a woman who was to acquire almost legendary status in Welsh tradition because of her beauty and charm. She was the daughter of Rhys ap Tewdwr of Deheubarth, the wife of Henry's steward, Gerald of Windsor and the grandmother of Giraldus Cambrensis. Henry I himself became the father of one of her many children. It was an attempt by the Bishop of London on the king's behalf to use Madog ap Rhiryd and his brother Ithel to punish Owain for his actions which led to the complex chain of events that resulted in Madog's brutal murder of Iorwerth ap Bleddyn. In 1116 Henry I sent Owain to campaign in south Wales. There he was tracked down and killed in battle by a party of Flemings led by Gerald of Windsor, who thus had his revenge for Owain's treatment of Nest.[4]

After Owain ap Cadwgan's death, his lands were split up between his six brothers, leaving Powys even more fragmented. Then in 1121 Henry I attacked. Maredudd ap Bleddyn sent a handful of young archers to shoot at the English army as they came along a wooded slope near the border. One of their arrows hit the king himself. It was deflected by his armour and he was physically unharmed, but the experience terrified

Henry. He made peace with Maredudd and Cadwgan's sons and withdrew his army.[5] Soon however there was conflict between Gwynedd and Powys. The family troubles also continued. Maredudd was present when his son Gruffudd killed his first cousin, Ithel ap Rhiryd ap Bleddyn (brother of the late and unlamented Madog ap Rhiryd) in 1125. In the same year Morgan ap Cadwgan (one of Owain's brothers) killed his brother Maredudd ap Cadwgan. As a penance, he had to go to Jerusalem as a crusader. He died in Cyprus on his way home in 1128. In the same year Maredudd ap Bleddyn's violent son Gruffudd also died.[6]

Gradually Powys was coming back under the control of Maredudd ap Bleddyn. In 1132 he himself died. Maredudd earned the praise of the *Brut* chronicler, who described him as 'the splendour and defence of the men of Powys.' He said that Maredudd died 'after having done penance on his soul and body and worthily receiving the Body of Christ.'[7] The dead prince was succeeded by his son Madog ap Maredudd. Powys was at last united and at peace. Even the chronicler had to note that 'in the four years after that . . . there was nothing that might be placed on record.'[8] No history was good history as far as Powys was concerned.

Madog ap Maredudd's rule was to be remembered as the golden age of Powys. After the hideous feuds and murders of the preceding decades there was now a remarkable degree of peace and stability, even if Madog did come under pressure from his aggressive and ambitious neighbour Owain Gwynedd from time to time. The author of *Breuddwyd Rhonabwy* ('The Dream of Rhonabwy'), which will be discussed later, summed up the memory of that time in his opening sentences: 'Madog ap Maredudd was ruler of Powys within its borders. That is from Porffordd to Gwafan in Arwystli.'[9] For a brief and glorious period in history, the fragmented land was whole again. He actually managed to expand its borders for a time. From 1149 to 1157 Madog even added the lordship of Oswestry to his territory, building a castle there.[10]

Powys now had a ruler and a court. Madog's principal court was at Mathrafal to the south-west of Meifod. A court required a poet. Madog ap Maredudd was to become the first patron of a son of Powys who would be the most prolific of all the poets of the Welsh princes: Cynddelw Brydydd Mawr. We have already come across him as the poet who sang the praises of St Tysilio and the religious community at Meifod. He was known as 'Cynddelw the Great Poet'. There is a suggestion that the epithet *Mawr* (which can also mean 'big') might have applied to Cynddelw's physical size or his reputation as chief poet. It might just as well have described his ego. He was a proud, self-assured man, confident of his privileged status as the leading court poet in Wales. Even in his earliest poems to Madog ap Maredudd this is clear:

> I praise a lord with the nine parts of my art,
> With nine inspirations and nine sorts of singing,
> Praising a brave man who has Gogrfran's courage,
> The noise of the deluge that sweeps away the shore.
> Red-speared in a strong army, Cadfan's handsome son,
> Long may the chief of men reign over us.
> Lord of campaigning, perfect leader,
> Powerful Madog, knight on the battlefield,
> My poetry is not incomplete on earth,
> My song is not shameful or powerless beside you.
> Eager for war, to win a fortress or a splendid battlefield,
> Thick around a courageous lion, a sharer of shining silver,
> Is the crowd around him scrambling for gifts at New Year,
> Like a bubbling wave's excitement on a beach around a sea gull's feet.
> Wanderer in the safety of the craft of my poetry
> (He is honoured by fair praise that shall not disappear)
> Patron to a stranger, with a broken shield,
> I drank in your court, most perfect of Powysmen,
> Honourable drink from a splendid cup,
> From gilded drinking horns, dignified drinking horns.
> You always gave us little horses
> Long leaping beneath a flag,
> Piebald, smooth-haired, shaped like deer from rich pastures,
> The colour of blue-grey fish, young sea salmon.
> His blood-soaked hand winning praise on the battlefield,
> An eagle ruling lords since he was first a chieftain.
> In the vanguard with a javelin on sure-footed steeds,
> A pursuer, a leader, a wolf in his fury.
> My sure passion for my strong exalted prince is lovely,
> Let me sing – what shall I sing? Famous wounder in battle:
> I sing because I love (since what I say is sublime)
> Singing a poem in exchange for food at a praiseworthy man's door;
> Get up, sing, I shall sing my poem,
> And I shall go in, poets, and you will go out![11]

Cynddelw was full of unshakeable self-confidence as he showed his fellow poets the door.

However there was one group of people in Madog's retinue who get the better of the bombastic poet. Efa, Madog ap Maredudd's daughter, and her handmaidens were more than a match for the 'Great Poet', as he ruefully admitted in a poem that Ann Parry Owen suggests was probably composed to be sung as light entertainment at court:

> Lively eager stallion, I greatly desire
> The one I praise and have praised before.
> A girl white as foam on water that the wind blows away,
> A quiet, fluent Welsh speaker from the court in the valley:
> Shining like the dawn light at the break of day,
> The same colour as bright white snow on the slopes of Epynt;
> Never too familiar, with shining eyes,
> She doesn't think much of me, though others think a lot of me.
> Her maidens were talking to her,
> And praised my 'Maidensong for Efa'.
> They kept to their chamber
> On a journey when I visited
> The place where Powys soldiers gather;
> When I sought permission to go
> To the place where they were,
> They watched me through glass windows:
> Shining sea gulls stared at me,
> They sent an answer that made me fade away.
> I would love them happily, though they wouldn't love me,
> They were chaste, innocent handmaidens,
> Considering at length the wisest thing to do,
> They were thinking about Cynddelw the poet![12]

It wasn't only Efa's handmaidens who spurned Cynddelw and sent him into a deep decline. The princess herself also ignored the 'Great Poet'. He was eloquent about his misery:

> Lively eager stallion, prepare to go
> (Look over to the court of the Powysmen, her relatives!)
> To a court where noblemen stroll around:
> The court of Efa who was made for the sake of poets,
> Her tall body is courtly in its golden mantle,

Modest blessed wise girl, as beautiful as white foam;
Brave warriors flock to a lady who is meant to be proud,
The colour of broken foam in front of the ninth wave.
No one has suffered since it began,
A ninth part of my pain, or anything like it!
I don't count it good for a girl to be mean:
It's not praiseworthy to reject me since I'm so good!
And say there about the affliction that's come upon me
And come back to me with a favourable answer,
And for my sake don't pretend that you haven't seen me,
And that I'm in anguish because she doesn't trust me,
And for your own good, don't let me be doubted!
And for the Lord of heaven's sake, don't let me be scorned!
She snubbed me before sending me away,
I'd accept her pity if she would give it;
I'm her obedient poet by right,
But I never get a kind word from her;
Though she may not love me, may she never blame me:
If she blamed me, may she never deprive me of her protection.[13]

This is only part of a long and entertaining poem that must have been enthusiastically received in the great hall at Mathrafal. It conveys something of the lively humour of Madog ap Maredudd's court. After the years of savagery and brutality there was finally an opportunity for relaxation and enjoyment.

It was too good to last long. In 1160, after a reign that had lasted twenty-eight years, Madog ap Maredudd of Powys died. The *Brut* chronicler was generous in praise of a ruler whom he described as 'a man of great praise, whom God had formed with physical beauty and fashioned with wisdom untold, and filled with doughtiness and adorned with generosity. He was generous and kind and meek toward the poor, and the meek, and harsh and unkind towards the warlike mighty.' Madog was buried in the church of St Tysilio at Meifod.[14] Cynddelw composed an elegy for him:

I ask my Lord for the confidence of a gift,
I ask, I have asked a hundred times,
To try to shape a splendid song in my best language
For my lord and friend,
To lament for Madog, giver of feasts and mead, who has mourners

And enemies in every country:
Guardian of the fortress, bearer of the shield,
Like a shield in attack, in a splendid battle,
Like the sound of burning heather in a tumult,
Scatterer of the enemy, defender in a conflict.
Chieftain sung countless songs, hope of the poets,
A blood-soaked companion, unhindered, unbending.
Before his death Madog was called
A netter of villainous loathsome enemies!
Generous to me, answer to my hope,
Unsparingly giving clothes and Gascon horses;
He bore the blood-stained spear of Brân fab Llyr Llediaith,
He was generously praised for heaping up spoils,
He didn't avoid bloodthirsty destroyers,
A constant giver, a holder of hostages,
His blade brought fear in battle and conflict,
A blade dipped in blood, that he was proud to fight with,
A swift hand beneath a many coloured shield,
Lord of Powys, a land that's lost hope now;
A demander of his rights, not playing at soldiering,
Brave thoughout his life, defender of four nations,
Of royal lineage in ancient iron armour,
Generous Madog, terrifier of his enemies,
Since he has died, we've died because of his death,
Since he has gone, a friend has gone!
He liked poets who wrote finely wrought poetry,
He was a strong anchor on a deep wild sea,
He welcomed abundantly, he was generous, beloved,
His fighting led to noisy battles;
A giver of drinking horns, an upholder of his royal rights,
A splendid lion from Cadiaith's royal line;
A strong and faultless friend of chieftains,
His fists wore iron armour, he wore an iron crown.
May his end, since his death has happened,
Pay recompense for so much injustice that results from it,
In the light of the saints, on a shining journey,
In the blessed light of perfect freedom.[15]

Cynddelw wrote the things that a court poet was supposed to write about his dead prince. Courage in battle (with plenty of references to blood), generosity to poets and a certainty of the bliss of heaven were the three essential elements. Nevertheless there does seem a note of genuine affection in the poem. Madog ap Maredudd had provided stability and hope after some particularly desperate years. The chronicler noted that Llywelyn ap Madog, 'his son, in whom lay the hope of all Powys,' was killed not long after his father's funeral.[16] Cynddelw wrote a second lament, mourning both the father and the son:

> May God leave no man alive any more,
> He has put them in two graves,
> The death of Madog is a great sadness to me,
> The killing of Llywelyn is complete destruction![17]

Powys had begun to unravel again.

ii) Owain Cyfeiliog

Without Llywelyn ap Madog to hold it together, Powys was split up once again. The northern part was divided between Gruffydd ap Madog (Gruffydd Maelor I), his brother Owain Fychan ap Madog ap Maredudd and their illegitimate half-brother, Owain Brogyntyn. Iorwerth Goch ap Maredudd, Madog's distinctly dodgy half-brother, also had a small share.[18] In the south the dominant figure was Owain Cyfeiliog, the son of Madog ap Maredudd's brother, Gruffudd. Owain Cyfeiliog had established a considerable reputation as a border raider in his youth. He even appears in a late thirteenth-century Anglo-Norman romance, *Fouke le Fitz Waryn*, as a courageous knight who severely wounds the hero of the story (whose family held lands in Shropshire).[19]

Owain's early exploits may have been the reason why he and his brother Meurig were entrusted with the western commote of Cyfeiliog by Madog ap Maredudd in 1149. It was an area that was probably the most sensitive and vulnerable of Madog's domains, bordering on the lands of both Owain Gwynedd and the Lord Rhys of Deheubarth. Owain Cyfeiliog's first wife was Gwenllian, Owain Gwynedd's daughter, which may have helped to ease the pressure from the north a little. However the Lord Rhys remained a threat and in 1153 he devastated Cyfeiliog. He would continue to claim the commote after Madog ap Maredudd's death, while Owain Gwynedd would also occupy parts of it.

At some time in the 1150s Owain built a castle in the township of Trallwng Llywelyn (Welshpool) and established his headquarters there.

After he took over southern Powys in 1160, he became involved in the developing conflict between the Welsh princes and Henry II. Owain and two of his cousins joined together to capture the royal castle of Carreghofa near Llanymynech in 1163. Two years later he was one of the Welsh princes who came together in a united army at Corwen to resist Henry's invasion. The following year Owain and his cousin Owain Fychan drove their uncle Iorwerth Goch out of his territory of Mochnant and divided it between them. [20]

Then in 1167 a major crisis developed. Owain Gwynedd, his brother Cadwaladr and the Lord Rhys united to attack southern Powys, with the collusion of Owain Fychan ap Madog ap Maredudd, who received Caereinion in exchange for his support. Owain Cyfeiliog was forced to escape over the border and do a deal with Henry. He came back with a Norman army and liberated his occupied possessions, burning down the brand new castle that his cousin had just built at Caereinion and slaughtering its garrison. [21] This experience left its mark on Owain for the rest of his career. He would never again trust the rulers of Gwynedd or Deheubarth, or indeed his cousin Owain Fychan. From 1167 he became a staunch ally of the king of England as the only person he could depend on to ensure his survival. It may be that it was as a sign of thanks to God for his restoration to his lands that Owain endowed the Cistercian monastery of Ystrad Marchell near Welshpool in 1170.

One rather improbable admirer of the mature Owain Cyfeiliog was Giraldus Cambrensis. When Baldwin, Archbishop of Canterbury, went around Wales in 1188 to collect recruits for the Third Crusade, all the Welsh princes came to offer their support except Owain. It may be that his disillusionment with his fellow Welsh rulers had reached such a pitch by then that he automatically boycotted anything that had their backing. Baldwin was not impressed and excommunicated Owain Cyfeiliog. Having recorded this in his account of their journey, Giraldus goes on to give a glowing description of the prince of southern Powys, describing him as 'more fluent in speech than the other Welsh princes' and 'well known for the sensible way in which he managed his land.' He also lists him as one of three Welsh rulers who have governed with 'equity, prudence and princely moderation.'

Giraldus's positive view of Owain Cyfeiliog was influenced by the way in which the prince handled his friendship with King Henry II. He tells

a story which shows that Owain was not prepared to flatter his powerful
ally. When the two of them were sitting at table in Shrewsbury one day,
Henry handed his Welsh ally one of the royal loaves as a special mark of
his favour. Owain took the loaf and carefully and deliberately started to
break it into pieces as though he was a priest preparing to distribute
Holy Communion. Then, with the king watching him intently, he put
the pieces in a row and slowly began to eat them one at a time, again
giving the impression that he was at a Communion service. When he had
finished, King Henry asked him what on earth he was doing. 'I am
imitating you, my lord,' came the reply. Giraldus explains that Owain's
charade was a subtle dig at Henry's habit of keeping church benefices
empty for as long as possible so that their revenue would go into the
royal coffers. This combination of witty independence of spirit and
defence of church interests clearly appealed to the Cambro–Norman
ecclesiastic.[22]

Owain's alliance with Henry ensured his security for the rest of his
days. The aging prince gradually transferred his lands to his son
Gwenwynwyn and eventually abdicated altogether. He spent his final
years as monk in the monastery that he had founded at Ystrad Marchell,
and it was there that he was buried on his death in 1197. The epitaph on
his tombstone described him as 'a respecter of the church' and an
'attacker of enemies'.[23] His fickle cousin, Owain Fychan ap Madog had
come to a less peaceful end ten years earlier. The chronicler recorded that
he was killed at Carreghofa near Llanymynech 'through treachery by
night' by Owain Cyfeiliog's sons, Gwenwynwyn and Cadwallon.[24]

Poets and princes had a symbiotic relationship in twelfth-century
Wales. The poet needed a prince to look after him, supplying him with
food, drink, clothes and a horse to ride. The prince needed a poet to sing
his praises and maintain his reputation. After the death of Madog ap
Maredudd, the 'Great Poet' had to look for a suitably big ruler to support
him. Cynddelw had already established himself as a major bard who
would be an ornament to any princely court. For the next ten years he
sang the praises of Madog's great rival, Owain Gwynedd. He would later
be willing to travel south to offer his services to the Lord Rhys, the last
great ruler of Deheubarth.

However Cynddelw also maintained his relationship with Powys. He
composed poems for the wealthy Powys landowner Rhirid Flaidd, for

Owain Fychan ap Madog ap Maredudd and for Owain Cyfeiliog's son and successor, Gwenwynwyn. He even sang a rather formal lament for the highly questionable Iorwerth Goch ap Maredudd, giving the wholly misleading impression that his subject had been 'Lord-chieftain over the beautiful land of Powys' (presumably Iorwerth's family gave him a hefty reward for making such an outrageously inaccurate claim). Most importantly he wrote two songs in praise of Owain Cyfeiliog himself.[25]

Owain Cyfeiliog seems to have had a deep interest in poetry. Indeed it has been long suggested that the prince was a poet himself, steeped in the heroic tradition of the earliest Welsh literature. Two poems have been attributed to him: *'Hirlas Owain'* ('Owain's Drinking Horn') and *'Englynion cylchu Cymru'* ('Verses about going round Wales').[26] Recently however Gruffydd Aled Williams has persuasively argued on the basis of a detailed analysis of their contents that the real author of these poems was actually Cynddelw Brydydd Mawr. He suggests that Cynddelw wrote them as a dramatic exercise in the tradition of the earlier poetry of Powys, with the prince speaking through his poet.[27]

The *Hirlas* was written to celebrate one of Owain's more dramatic exploits. In 1156 he led his war-band northwards into Maelor to rescue his brother Meurig who was being held prisoner there by the Norman earl of Chester. The poem celebrates the return of Owain's warriors having successfully carried out their mission. It is full of echoes of the *Gododdin*, Aneirin's heroic epic which was written around the year 600. The *Gododdin* had described how an army of warriors drawn from all the remaining British/Welsh territories had been recruited by Mynyddog Mwynfawr, ruler of an area around what is now Edinburgh, to attack the invading Angles. The war-band rode 150 miles south to Catraeth (now Catterick in north Yorkshire). There they were almost completely wiped out by their enemies. The poet survived to return to the court and describe the heroism of those who died.[28] The important difference between the *Gododdin* and the *Hirlas* is that the latter describes a glorious victory rather than a shattering defeat.

Owain Cyfeiliog is the speaker in the *Hirlas*. The warriors are gathered together in his castle at Welshpool to celebrate the success of the raid. He calls on his long-suffering cup-bearer to pass the drinking-horn to his men in turn to drink to their personal valour. An atmosphere of cheerful booziness prevails:

Readily pass the drinking-horn, cup-bearer,
To the hand of Rhys in the giver's court:
Owain's court always fed with spoils,
They feed a thousand, the doors are open.
Cup-bearer, may I not be quiet:
Bring me the vessel, coloured like the ninth wave,
Shaped like a horn, covered in gold,
To drink, full of longing, with my war-band.
Put more bragget of beer and mead
In the hand of strong Gwgon for his deed.
Goronwy's cubs, powerful in battle's excitement,
Strong cubs, their actions brave,
Men who deserve their payment in each battle,
Valiant rescuers, valuable in a fight:
Severn's defenders, glad to hear
The noise of drinking-horns generously full.

Pass the horn to Cynfelyn who's made
Honourably drunk by the foaming mead,
And if you want to live for another year,
Don't refuse him respect, that wouldn't be proper . . .[29]

Occasionally the mood becomes more sombre, as the prince remembers those members of his war-band who had been killed during the expedition. The blustering becomes somewhat maudlin as Owain laments his fallen companions:

Cup-bearer, pass (unless you want death),
The horn with honour in the feasts,
The drinking-horn made from a wild ox horn, honoured tonight,
The silver that covers it isn't insubstantial.
Give Tudur, eagle of battles,
The first drink of the brown wine
(Unless a cup of the best mead of all
Comes in, you'll be executed!)
And to Moriddig, patron of poems
That spread his praise before his sad burial.
Brave brothers, noble men,
Courageous under their shields.
Warriors who served me faithfully,
Always the same, never fickle.

Warriors, wolves, attacking in the vanguard,
With bloody spears in the battlefield's fury.
Courageous brave men from Mochnant in Powys
Both of them wildly keen to fight,
Red-weaponed attackers in every battle,
They guarded their borders from trouble.
Those I've just named deserve to be praised;
They're lamented now that they both are dead.
Oh Christ, the sorrow makes me so sad!
Losing Moriddig, so greatly missed.[30]

The dramatic quality of the poem is quite startling. The drunken prince comes alive, slurring his words as he points across the table towards his companions, or bullies the wretched cup-bearer, or wipes away a tear as he remembers a dead friend. And there is a wonderful moment when he recalls the victory and the glorious scene as the warriors galloped along the banks of the Severn in the sunshine, heading for home.

A brave man met with an army of enemies:
A steward was killed, a fortress burned near the shoreline.
We rescued a very valuable prisoner:
Meurig ap Gruffudd of powerful destiny.
Everyone was sweating when they returned:
The Long Mountain and the valley were full of sun.[31]

The poet cannot help gloating as he compares their success with the abject failure of the heroes of the *Gododdin*:

I heard that a war-band went to Catraeth for a payment of mead,
They were properly armed and their weapons were sharp.
Mynyddog's retinue was praised for dying,
As front-line fighters frightening the enemy.
My warriors did no worse in the battle in Maelor,
Releasing a prisoner in a praiseworthy way.[32]

The other poem ascribed to Owain is something of a wild romp and was apparently written to amuse his household at a New Year feast.[33] It is a series of verses addressed, not to the cup-bearer, but to another servant who is ordered to gallop around north Wales to warn people that Owain and his retinue are on their way and that suitable food and lodging should be provided for them. Part of the joke behind the poem is the blithe assumption that Owain is actually the ruler not just of southern Powys but of the whole of north Wales.

The servant is to start at Ffordun (Forden, on the border not far from Owain's castle at Welshpool), go south to Ceri (Kerry east of Newtown), westward to Arwystli (the Llanidloes area) and on to Penweddig (the northernmost part of Ceredigion around Llanbadarn Fawr). From there he is to head northwards along the coast through Meirionnydd and Ardudwy to Llŷn. The verse about Llŷn contains a reference to one of Owain's many girlfriends, and doubtless raised a guffaw from the assembled company:

> Start off, messenger, to the beautiful limit of the land
> That Merfyn governed;
> Go to stay with Nest of Nefyn,
> Tell her that we are coming to Llŷn.[34]

The messenger has to gallop onwards to Arfon and Môn (Anglesey) and then back eastwards to Rhos in Gwynedd Is Conwy, Llannerch in Dyffryn Clwyd, Tynobydwal in Bryneglwys yn Iâl, Maelor, Cynllaith, Mechain and home. The journey ends with a breathless finale:

> Lord Owain's retinue, we've offended the lands on earth:
> May the land of heaven be our dwelling place.
> We've been on an easy, swift, successful raid,
> We've made a circuit around Wales.[35]

And no doubt the galloping around was acted out by Owain and his men as part of their New Year festivities.

As well as the two poems which were either written by Owain Cyfeiliog or by Cynddelw Brydydd Mawr in Owain's name, there are two more poems addressed directly by Cynddelw to the prince.[36] One of them concentrates on Owain as a warrior:

> His round shield is strong as he strolls around armies,
> He can make loud and threatening sounds,
> A perfect killer coming smiling from battle
> With a broken bloodstained blade, he shares gifts to satisfy us;
> A strong and powerful protector, used to packs of wolves
> Devouring dead men's flesh in many a valley,
> Generous hearted, causing much pain to an enemy,
> Guarding his homeland with strong sincerity.[37]

Cynddelw's poem provides evidence of some border skirmishes from Owain's earlier years that were not included among the events recorded in the *Brut*. It speaks of battles with the English/Normans. One was at Cawres or Caus Castle on the Shropshire side of the Long Mountain. This belonged to the Fitz Warins and the reference is presumably to the fight that later earned Owain his place in the Anglo-Norman romance mentioned above. Others were at Ffordun (Forden), Gwestun (Weston Madoc, just north of Church Stoke in Montgomeryshire), Melltun (Mellington near Church Stoke), Trefalun (probably Allington, north-east of Wrexham) and Llidwm (now Lydham, north-east of Bishop's Castle in Shropshire). Owain is described as 'the defender of the stronghold of Dygen' (the Breidden hills north of the Long Mountain or Mynydd Digoll) and as 'destruction to a host of men on the banks of the Severn.' He is clearly portrayed as the highly effective guardian of the borderland.

The other poem, which focuses on Owain's generosity in his court at Welshpool, is also laced with references to the border area:

> So frequently I've received Owain's drink,
> Over beyond Mynydd Digoll,
> Splendid wine, it's no loss to drink it,
> And mead from all the drinking horns . . .

> Generous Owain's drink, happily given,
> In the district beside the Severn,
> It's an attractive provision indeed,
> Coming from beyond Dygen . . .

> Drink welcomes us in starlight and moonlight,
> From a generous leader with a bloodstained spear,
> Around the Long Mountain[38] is a tall strong lord,
> Around the lovely Severn men are smiling.[39]

In the end Owain grew weary of the bloodstained blades, the endless carousing and the heavy-handed flattery of the 'Great Poet'. The peaceful cloisters of Ystrad Marchell alongside the river in a part of Wales that he had defended so successfully became a quiet sanctuary where he could prepare himself for the life to come. At the end of the drunken flourishes of the *Hirlas*, he (or the poet who spoke for him) had caught a glimpse of something better than the fame to be won from battles as the drinking horn suddenly seemed transformed into a chalice – a Holy Grail:

> Cup-bearer, don't refuse me, let me not be rejected;
> May we be welcomed in paradise.
> May we have a long welcome from the Chieftain of kings,
> Where true safety can be seen.[40]

Tysilio, another prince of Powys turned monk, would have understood.

iii) Cynddelw meets his God

Cynddelw was growing old. As a young man he had astonished the court of Madog ap Maredudd, driving all the other poets from the hall. In his prime he had sung to the great lords of the north and south, Owain Gwynedd and the Lord Rhys, as well as joining in the hi-jinks of the *hirlas* with his special patron and friend, Owain Cyfeiliog. Now Owain had gone and the 'Great Poet' was called on to sing to Gwenwynwyn ab Owain Cyfeiliog, representative of a third generation of the princes of Powys.

Gwenwynwyn tried his best – but he was not his father. His only lasting achievement would be a geographical one. He would bequeath his name to the southern part of Powys so that, until the creation of Montgomeryshire, it became known as 'Powys Wenwynwyn'. His first crisis came in 1196, a year after he had assumed complete control and while his father was still alive in the monastery at Ystrad Marchell. Owain Cyfeiliog's careful alliance had collapsed, and the archbishop of Canterbury (of all people!) beseiged Gwenwynwyn in his castle at Welshpool.

Archbishop Henry had the support of an alliance of English earls and barons 'and the princes of Gwynedd,' the chronicler informs us. The archbishop's men were armed with all the most up-to-date siege equipment. Eventually his sappers succeeded in tunnelling under the walls and Gwenwynwyn and his garrison were forced to surrender. Their lives and their weapons were spared, and within the year the prince won back the castle that had been his father's headquarters for so many years. Even so, it was hardly a very auspicious beginning to his reign.[41]

For a time things did improve. The Lord Rhys of Deheubarth died in 1197. Gwenwynwyn took advantage of a dispute over the succession and as a result gained Arwystli. This boosted his confidence. The upset in Deheubarth and internal dynastic squabbles in Gwynedd had created a temporary power vacuum in Wales. Gwenwynwyn therefore took on the role of the leading Welsh prince, gathered a huge army and in 1198 attacked the lands of the marcher lords, laying siege to Painscastle, which was eventually captured. The English counterattacked and inflicted a massive defeat on Gwenwynwyn and his allies.[42]

In the years that followed, Llywelyn ap Iorwerth of Gwynedd began to emerge as the leading figure in Wales and Gwenwynwyn was forced to make concessions to him. Then in 1208 King John seized the prince of southern Powys at Shrewsbury. For the next two years Llywelyn occupied Gwenwynwyn's lands until the English king relented and restored them to him. Gwenwynwyn was now caught between the rulers of Gwynedd and England. If he favoured one, he automatically offended the other and put himself and his territory in danger. In 1211 King John forced him to join in a campaign against Llywelyn ap Iorwerth. In the following year he was coerced into an alliance with Llywelyn and eventually swore an oath of homage to him in 1215 (the year when the English king was embroiled in the domestic troubles which led to the signing of Magna Carta), joining him on his successful campaign in south Wales.

In 1216 Gwenwynwyn made one last desperate attempt to assert himself as an alternative Welsh leader. He broke the oath he had made to Llywelyn and made peace with King John. It was a disastrous mistake. Llywelyn invaded and occupied southern Powys. Gwenwynwyn had to abandon everything and seek refuge over the border. He died an exile in Cheshire, leaving two infant sons.[43] For the next quarter of a century Powys Wenwynwyn was under the thumb of the princes of Gwynedd. It was not until 1241 that Gruffydd ap Gwenwynwyn was restored to his father's territory by King Henry III.[44]

But that was all in the future. Cynddelw did not survive to see very much of Gwenwynwyn ab Owain Cyfeiliog's unhappy reign. He did however compose three poems of praise to the new ruler.[45] They are rather mechanical exercises, saying the right things (as always), but the spark and the enthusiasm have gone. The old poet was beginning to lose interest in earthly rulers. Years before he had sung the praises of Tysilio's monastery at Meifod. Now that he began to think about his final resting-place, he did not seek it in the ancient monastic enclosure of Gwyddfarch and his princely disciple. It was true that the great Madog ap Maredudd had been buried at Meifod, but times had changed. Owain Cyfeiliog had been buried in Ystrad Marchell, the Cistercian monastery that he had founded and of which he had eventually become a member. Cynddelw decided that it was only fitting that the prince's chief poet should rest alongside him.

The bard therefore sent a request that he himself might spend his last days at Ystrad Marchell and be buried there. A monk from the abbey brought him the reply. It was in the negative. It may be that someone remembered Cynddelw's powerful poem in praise of the community at Meifod and felt a certain amount of jealousy. It may be that the Cistercians of Ystrad Marchell were rather suspicious of poets at this time (they would later become famous for their hospitality towards them). Whatever the reason, Cynddelw was disappointed and he responded with a sad but dignified little verse:

> Although there was no agreement to receive and let me in,
> As holy God knows,
> It would be more fitting for a monk
> To welcome me than refuse me.[46]

Perhaps the verse had its desired effect and the poet was allowed to find a final refuge in the monastery that had meant so much to his prince. Or it may be that Cynddelw had to go elsewhere for succour and support. Somehow he acquired the time and space to write his *Marwysgafn*: the 'deathbed poem' through which the bard had to sing himself into heaven.

Even before that final composition Cynddelw had begun to redirect the persuasive powers that he had developed in a lifetime of praising self-important princes towards winning the favour of the greatest ruler of all. He had already produced two substantial poems addressed to God.[47] The first of them began almost as if the poet was singing to an omnipotent version of Madog ap Maredudd:

> One powerful Lord, a Prince fond of justice,
> Reigns without anxiety,
> One Son of God with an immense purpose,

One Son of Mary, strong, invincible,
One eternal and merciful God,
One King, Chieftain of heaven and earth,
One Hero, whose purpose is heroic,
I wish to give him a holy song through gentle prayer.
Let me be my Lord's friend before death's danger,
Let me become more penitent for my sins.[48]

Cynddelw, like all his medieval contemporaries, was very much aware of the stark reality of death. He also desperately desired a place in a heavenly court whose King had the power to be more generous than any of the rulers that the poet had flattered over the years:

Before I become a poor beggar in need
My life full of worry, my old body clumsy,
Before the necessity of pitiless death,
Painful wretchedness and the green covered earth,
Before the terrible moment of separation,
Before I'm taken to the final prison,
Before the grave's sad wretched affliction, confined
In a covering of oak and blood,
Dignified King of abundant laws, gentle Lord,
King and Judge, Sharer of kind tokens,
Generous Saviour scattering gifts
To supplicants, Giver of wonderful presents,
It's fitting that I through my learned and eloquent power
Should praise without ceasing, sparing no loveliness;
I'm a supplicant full of passion and sorrow,
I pray to God to atone for His anger.[49]

For the poet the alternative to winning God's favour was utterly terrifying. The pains of hell had a concrete reality for Cynddelw: they involved freezing marshes, endless wailing, leaping flames, uncontrollable desires, profound depression and an appalling sense of shame exacerbated by hideous demonic tormentors. However he remained confident that his poetic gifts were sufficient to win God's patronage:

After the New Year's gift and the lovely festival
When brave men are fed around the drinking vessel,
After love and weapons and graceful white stallions,
Properly fed war horses from a refined court,

After a payment like the one in St John's declaration,
Before a grave under green turf, before my face goes pale,
God will give me, because of the gift of my craft,
Easy confidence as I work in the vineyard,
Then when utterly terrifying judgement comes,
May my place be on my Lord's right hand![50]

In his second poem to God, while talking of the vanity of human desires and attainments, Cynddelw listed the great heroes of the past: Arthur, Julius Caesar, Brân ap Llyr, Hercules and Alexander. A name that was also included was Madog, 'the praiseworthy leader' – who might be (as Marged Haycock has suggested) King Arthur's brother, Madog ap Uthr, but must otherwise be Madog ap Maredudd, the poet's first patron.[51] Cynddelw's confidence came through at the end of this poem as well, despite some doubts about his past frivolousness:

I pray through Mary's intercession for peace before death,
That my joking may not cause me painful harm,
Before pitifully entering my home in the earth,
Paying God that which is due to him.
With a legion of angels, a nation's fair hope,
Before death and in front of a vast gathering,
May I be blessed by praising Christ the Lord,
And find safety in the dwelling place of the nine heavens.[52]

These were in a sense practice pieces for Cynddelw's last great effort: the poem that he composed as he was dying.[53] This genre was part of the tradition of the poets of the princes and 'deathbed poems' by Meilyr Brydydd and Bleddyn Fardd have also survived.[54] The poem is a confession in which the poet seeks to be reconciled to God, receiving forgiveness and acceptance into heaven. It is the single most important work that he has to produce in his lifetime: his passport to eternity.

The dying Cynddelw began his poem with an attractive description of God's creative generosity:

I ask, God, for a fitting change of heart
To help me praise my generous, blessed King,
Mary's Only Son who makes afternoon, morning
And powerful estuaries,
Who created trees and fields of suitable size,

Crops and gifts, all made by God;
Who created grass and bushes and mountain heather,
And made some men happy by fair judgement
And others, lost by a rejected blessing,
Needy and indignant.
I ask God's Son, because he will fulfil it,
For reconciliation for our sins and wrong doing,
And welcome in the heaven our sanctuary:
We shall go to the land that we desire![55]

With God's help he can produce praise that will echo that of the angelic
host, and therefore make him a poet worthy enough to sing in the court
of his eternal Chieftain:

I ask, God, I request an excellent praise poem
That I can sing in metre;
Thousands praise you, Chieftain,
From among your hosts in your heighest height.
I would like, my Lord, to have it by your permission,
I believe in you through your love;
You are my patron, praiseworthy One,
Scatterer of gifts, don't let me go short!
More than necessary was the greatest blessing
Of the mighty Prince defending his furthest borders.
What I'm thinking of terrifies me
Because Adam sinned in the way he did.
I am a foolish exile living in your blessed land
With your splendid host around me;
They are the poets of the brightest church,
Their food has been shared with me.
My way is lovely, I'm aiming for a place,
I'm confident in my Chieftain, I seek his fellowship,
King of all nations, save me,
After wandering the world, may I receive good.
By permission of the most royal Father
And the Son and the Spirit, most shining holiness,
In the light of his privilege, may I be fortunate;
In the dwelling of chaste and gentlest angels,
In the Prince's blessed land, I ask for heaven.[56]

Cynddelw then outlines the history of salvation through Jesus Christ, expressing his faith and trust in him. The poet will repay his debt to his redeemer through poetry, and he is certain that this will be acceptable.

> Chief Prince, when you were born
> Mercy and salvation came to us,
> Adam's children came out from disbelief,
> From long transgression, from captivity;
> The one we desired came to visit us,
> Full, powerful courage came,
> Christ came in the flesh, Possessor of victory,
> The wished-for Son came in Mary's womb;
> Five ages of the world came out of terrible pain,
> From a place full of malice, darkness and deceit,
> From a painful existence, from deepest sorrow,
> They were released from the enemy's prison.
> He is our Leader, our complete protection
> Who judges our action according to our work;
> He, Lord of heaven, our peaceful destiny,
> Brought us from damnation when he was wounded;
> He will rise for us, his benefit will come to us,
> He's a King who will not hinder our good.
> He's a gift who was given
> Fully and strongly with endless authority.
> I shall give God a tithe from my hand
> Not holding back what is due to him.
> I am a poet, excellently formed,
> Under the patronage of my Creator, Prince of a multitude;
> May I, Cynddelw the singer, receive blessing,
> May Michael, who knows me, welcome me![57]

There is however no false modesty about Cynddelw. He is certain that God has created him to be a skilful and accomplished poet and that he has used this gift to his best ability. The poet admits that he has not set out to be an ascetic or a saint, but he has believed in God and used his art as a prayer for a place in heaven.

> Highest Prince, when I sang about you
> I didn't declaim a useless declamation;
> My poem didn't lack fine characteristics,
> From wherever I had it, my gift isn't meagre.

The steadfast God did not create me
To commit foolishness or deceit or violence.
Whoever believes in God doesn't lack religion,
He won't have to suffer a painful wound.
I didn't strive to keep awake to pray,
Heaven won't be given to those who don't seek it;
I didn't practise too much religious zeal,
I didn't deserve too great a prize.
The pride that I've nurtured in my heart isn't fitting,
I didn't think to suffer penance;
I've wished freedom for my soul in the Lord's dwelling-place,
I've prayed for what is necessary.[58]

His final great poem reaches its climax as Cynddelw brings all his powers of persuasion, honed by a lifetime of praising princely patrons, to bear on the only ruler who matters in the end:

Highest Prince, welcome
Worship as a greeting, as a perfect poem:
My flawless phrase has been created
As a song to praise you, Candle of a hundred lands.
Because you are the Possessor, the great Controller,
Because you are the Leader, the Lord of light,
Because you have a prophet's heart, because you are a Judge,
Because you are a generous King, because you are a Giver,
Because you are my Teacher don't banish me from your presence,
Your power and your beautiful kingdom;
Don't deprive me of your blessing, Creator Lord,
Don't humiliate me before a graceless company,
Don't hand me out a wretched territory,
Don't let me go among a dark, despised crowd of people.[59]

And that is how, God willing, Cynddelw Brydydd Mawr, the proudest of all the poets of Powys, sang his way into heaven.

NOTES

[1] *Brut*, p.35.

[2] *Brut*, pp.35-6.

[3] *Brut*, pp.36-7.

[4] *Brut*, pp.28-9, 44-5; *Dictionary of Welsh Biography*, p.683 ('Nest').

[5] *Brut*, pp.47-8.

[6] *Brut*, pp.49-50.

[7] *Brut*, p.50.

[8] *Brut*, p.51.

[9] Richards, *Breudwyt*, p.1.

[10] Davies, *Age of Conquest*, p.46; *Brut*, p.57.

[11] *Gwaith Cynddelw Brydydd Mawr*, I, 5.

[12] *Gwaith Cynddelw Brydydd Mawr*, I, 59.

[13] *Gwaith Cynddelw Brydydd Mawr* I, 60.

[14] *Brut*, p.61.

[15] *Gwaith Cynddelw Brydydd Mawr*, I, 87.

[16] *Brut*, p.62.

[17] *Gwaith Cynddelw Brydydd Mawr*, I, 96.

[18] For Iorwerth Goch ap Maredudd see *Gwaith Cynddelw Brydydd Mawr*, I, 143-4.

[19] '*Canu Owain Cyfeiliog*', edited by Gruffydd Aled Williams in *Gwaith Llywelyn Fardd I ac eraill o Feirdd y Ddeuddegfed Ganrif* (Cardiff, 1994), pp. 191-277 (pp.194-5).

[20] *Brut*, pp.62-4.

[21] *Brut*, p.64.

[22] Gerald, *Journey*, pp.202-3.

[23] '*Canu Owain Cyfeiliog*', p.197.

[24] *Brut*, p.73.

[25] *Gwaith Cynddelw Brydydd Mawr*, I, 143-249, 283-322.

[26] '*Canu Owain Cyfeiliog*', pp.221-66

[27] Gruffydd Aled Williams, 'Owain Cyfeiliog: Bardd-dywysog?' in *Beirdd a Thywysogion: Barddoniaeth Llys yng Nghymru, Iwerddon a'r Alban*, edited by Morfydd E. Owen and Brynley F. Roberts (Cardiff, 1996), pp.180-201.

[28] Williams, *Canu Aneirin*; Kenneth Hurlstone Jackson, *The Gododdin: The Oldest Scottish Poem* (Edinburgh, 1969); A.O.H. Jarman, *Aneirin: Y Gododdin – Britain's Oldest Heroic Poem* (Llandysul, 1988).

[29] '*Canu Owain Cyfeiliog*', p.226.

[30] '*Canu Owain Cyfeiliog*', p.227-8.

[31] '*Canu Owain Cyfeiliog*', p.228.

[32] '*Canu Owain Cyfeiliog*', p.229.

[33] This is suggested by the reference to '*Calan Ionawr*' in line 47 of the poem. Gruffydd Aled Williams, '*Canu Owain Cyfeiliog*', p.253 regards the poem as a flight of the imagination, written to entertain Owain's retinue.

[34] '*Canu Owain Cyfeiliog*', p.256

[35] '*Canu Owain Cyfeiliog*', p.257.

[36] *Gwaith Cynddelw Brydydd Mawr*, I, 185-228.

[37] *Gwaith Cynddelw Brydydd Mawr*, I, 190.

[38] Cynddelw (whether writing as himself or as Owain) has two names for the mountain. Wherever he calls it 'Mynydd Digoll' I have retained the Welsh name, wherever he uses 'Hirfryn' I have used the English 'Long Mountain'.

[39] *Gwaith Cynddelw Brydydd Mawr*, I, 224.

[40] '*Gwaith Owain Cyfeiliog*', p.229.

[41] *Brut*, p.76; A. D. Carr, 'Powys: Y Cefndir Hanesyddol yng Nghyfnod Beirdd y Tywysogion', *Llên Cymru* XXII (1999),12-24 (p.17).

[42] *Brut*, pp. 76-80.

[43] *Brut*, pp. 81-92; Carr, 'Powys: Y Cefndir Hanesyddol', p.18; *Dictionary of Welsh Biography*, p.325 ('Gwenwynwyn')

[44] Carr, 'Powys:Y Cefndir hanesyddol', p.19.

[45] *Gwaith Cynddelw Brydydd Mawr*, I, 229-49.

[46] *Gwaith Cynddelw Brydydd Mawr*, II, 257.

[47] *Gwaith Cynddelw Brydydd Mawr*, II, 261-325. For a recent translation of the two poems in their entirety and a detailed and valuable commentary on them see N.G. Costigan, *Defining the Divinity: Medieval Perceptions in Welsh Court Poetry* (Aberystwyth, 2002), pp.21-31, 81-8. Costigan comments wisely on the difficulties that face the translator of the first poem: 'Translation cannot convey the linguistic subtleties of this poem. It is too rich in flawless syntactic and grammatical expression, and in its variety of technique and careful choice of individual phrasing. The mere understanding of lines and couplets can on occasion challenge the expertise of even the most learned medieval Welsh scholars.'

[48] *Gwaith Cynddelw Brydydd Mawr*, II, 267.

[49] *Gwaith Cynddelw Brydydd* II, 267-8.

[50] *Gwaith Cynddelw Brydydd Mawr*, II, 272-3.

[51] *Gwaith Cynddelw Brydydd Mawr*, II, 321.

[52] *Gwaith Cynddelw Brydydd Mawr*, II, 308.

[53] *Gwaith Cynddelw Brydydd Mawr*, II, 326-48. For another recent translation see Catherine A. McKenna, *The Medieval Welsh Religious Lyric: Poems of the Gogynfeirdd, 1137-1282* (Belmont, Massachusetts, 1991), pp.164-9.

[54] *Gwaith Meilyr Brydydd a'i Ddisgynyddion*, edited by J.E. Caerwyn Williams and Peredur I. Lynch (Cardiff, 1994), pp.98-106; *Gwaith Bleddyn Fardd a Beirdd Eraill Ail Hanner y Drydedd Ganrif ar Ddeg*, edited by Rhian M. Andrews and others (Cardiff, 1996), pp.641-7.

[55] *Gwaith Cynddelw Brydydd Mawr*, II, 331.

[56] *Gwaith Cynddelw Brydydd Mawr*, II, 331-2.

[57] *Gwaith Cynddelw Brydydd Mawr*, II, 332.

[58] *Gwaith Cynddelw Brydydd Mawr*, II, 332-3.

[59] *Gwaith Cynddelw Brydydd Mawr*, II, 333.

5. RHONABWY'S DREAM AND GRUFFUDD LLWYD

i) *A Dream of Heroes*

Nobody knows who wrote the story called *Breuddwyd Rhonabwy* ('Rhonabwy's Dream').[1] It is thought that it most probably dates from the early thirteenth century and that it was composed during the bleak quarter century after Gwenwynwyn's death in exile when Powys Wenwynwyn ceased to exist.[2] The author of the poem clearly had a detailed knowledge of the geography of the area between Welshpool and the Long Mountain. It was this that led Enid Roberts to make the perceptive suggestion that the author might well have been one of the monks of Ystrad Marchell. As she pointed out, many of the places mentioned in the text would have been clearly visible to anyone who went for a stroll in the monastery garden.[3]

It is easy to understand why one of the monks of Ystrad Marchell might have felt disillusioned in the 1220s. The abbey had been founded by Owain Cyfeiliog, the heroic defender of the border. Every time he took part in a service in its church, the monk would have seen the tomb of the great prince of southern Powys. He may well have known the inscription on it off by heart, including the words '*Ecclesiae cultor . . . maior Owynus . . . hostibus insultor*' ('Respecter of the church . . . great Owain . . . attacker of enemies'). Owain's son, Gwenwynwyn, had tried his best to assist his father's monastery. Back in 1215 that same monk might well have been the scribe who copied out the last of the many charters recording grants of land from '*Wennunwen de Keueilliauc, dominus de Mungumeri*' to the abbey.[4] Now Gwenwynwyn was dead and Powys was no more. The only slender hope remaining was the possibility that an English king, fed up with the arrogance of Gwynedd, might consider restoring the child who was Gwenwynwyn's heir to his rightful inheritance. Yet, even around 1225, there must still have been a few old people alive who could just about remember the days when Powys had been a single united kingdom under the great Madog ap Maredudd, with his flourishing court at Mathrafal.

The monk must have thought long and deeply about this. Then he decided to write a story. It wouldn't be a heroic romance or a carefully crafted retelling of some ancient legend or folk tale. The writer wanted to surprise and shock his readers into thinking about what had happened to their corner of Wales. The story that he would tell would be a new one, even though it would be rooted in the past. He would tease the professional storytellers by proclaiming that it was too complicated to be remembered, and would always have to be read from a book. This was totally untrue: any storyteller worth his salt would quickly get the hang of it. He would also get in a dig at the pompous, bombastic bards as well. Most importantly he would try to make those who read or heard the story reconsider everything that they had ever been told about heroes. There would also be a political slant to the tale for those who wished to discern it. His story would be a masterpiece. Rhiannon Ifans recently described its author as 'a confident and intelligent man, fulfilling his achievement with the courage of his learning, in a very appropriate and amusing way.'[5]

The story begins in the days when Powys really was Powys – at the time when its borders from the top of Maelor to the bottom of Arwystli were under the control of Madog ap Maredudd. Madog had a brother who regarded himself as being extremely important and who became jealous of the king. This thorn in Madog's flesh was none other than the highly questionable Iorwerth Goch ap Maredudd, the subject of a rather improbable lament by Cynddelw Brydydd Mawr.[6] Madog offered his brother all sorts of honours and gifts and privileges, but nothing worked. Iorwerth still went raiding over the border into England, burning houses and taking hostages. This must have been particularly galling for Madog as he was trying to build up good relations with his eastern neighbours to counter the growing threat of Gwynedd in the west.

So, the storyteller informs us, Madog sent out parties of men to try to get hold of Iorwerth. One of the people taking part in this manhunt was called Rhonabwy. He and his companions were searching the border area along the river Vyrnwy in what was supposed to be one of the most prosperous parts of Powys. They reached the house of a man named Heilyn Goch son of Cadwgan son of Iddon and decided to stay for the night there. As is pointed out in a note to Melville Richards's edition of the story, there are two possible places where this house might have been. One is a Pentreheylin Hall on the banks of the Vyrnwy just west of Llandysilio, close to where the much fought-over border castle of Carreghofa once stood. A few miles to the east in the Shropshire parish of Kinnerley is another Pentreheylin Hall, also on the banks of the Vyrnwy.[7]

Whichever of the two Pentreheylins is the one in the story, it was not a pleasant place to be. The supposed prosperity of this part of the borderland was not reflected in the author's picture of Heilyn Goch's house. He described in graphic detail a scene of the utmost squalor. The building was obviously shared by people and animals. The floor was uneven, slippery with cow dung, with pools of cow's urine and water deep enough to cover a man's ankle. Stumps of holly whose twigs had been eaten by the cattle were scattered across it. When the guests came into the part of the hall meant for people, they found some bare, dusty sleeping platforms with an old hag keeping a fire going on one of them. Every time she began to feel cold, she would throw some chaff on it, producing the most awful stifling, choking smoke. On the other platform was a yellow heifer's skin.

When the visitors asked where Heilyn and his wife were, the old woman replied with insults. But then their hosts appeared: a half-bald, red-haired man with a wrinkled face and a bundle of twigs on his back, and a small, thin, pale woman, carrying a burden under her arm. They were less than thrilled to see the three men.

The woman lit a fire with the twigs and started baking, and then brought them a meal of barley bread and cheese, with watery skimmed milk to wash it down. Meanwhile there was a storm of wind and rain outside.

The visitors decided to abandon their journey for the time being and go to sleep. But when they looked at the sleeping shelf, they saw that the straw on it was short, dusty, flea-ridden and full of bits of twig. There was a threadbare, rough, red-grey blanket with holes in it stretched out over the straw and on the blanket was a torn, ragged sheet and an almost empty pillow with a filthy pillow-slip. Rhonabwy's two companions managed to doze off despite the fleas and the discomfort. But Rhonabwy himself was so uncomfortable that he decided to try the yellow heifer's skin. He lay down on it and went to sleep.

As soon as Rhonabwy closed his eyes, he imagined that he and his companions were crossing Maes Argyngroeg (Gungrog Fechan and Gungrog Fawr just north-east of Welshpool – Gungrog Fawr overlooks the site of Ystrad Marchell). They seemed to be heading for Rhyd-y-Groes-ar-Hafren, the ford across the river Severn near where Buttington Bridge now stands. As they travelled on Rhonabwy heard a noise unlike any noise that he had ever heard before. He looked back and saw a newly shaved young man with yellow curly hair on a yellow horse. The knight looked so ferocious that Rhonabwy and his companions ran away. He pursued them. His stallion's lungs was so powerful that when it breathed out the three men were pushed away from it and when it breathed in they were drawn close to it. Then the knight overtook them and they asked for his protection. He agreed and told them not to be afraid.

When they enquired who he was, he replied that he was Iddawg, son of Mynio, better known as Iddawg the Stirrer of Britain. He explained that he got his nickname from the time when he was sent by the emperor Arthur to make peace with Medrawd (Mordred). Arthur wanted to avoid the disaster of a destructive conflict with his nephew and foster-son. He couched his message in the gentlest language that he could find, but Iddawg passed his words on to Medrawd in the most offensive and insulting way possible. The result of Iddawg's stirring was the battle of Camlan. Iddawg went from there three nights before the end of the fighting and went to a place called the Llech Las to do seven year's penance for his disgraceful behaviour.

Then they heard an even greater noise and another young knight overtook them.

He demanded his share of the little men. At this point it becomes clear that all the people whom Rhonabwy and his companions meet in the dream are giants compared to themselves. After Iddawg got him to agree to become a second protector for the small strangers, the second knight rode away. They came nearer Rhyd-y-groes-ar-Hafren, which had been the scene of Gruffydd ap Llywelyn's great victory over the Mercians in 1039.[8] A mile from the ford, on both sides of the road, there were soldiers' huts and tents and a huge gathering of people.

Arthur himself was sitting on a flat meadow below the ford with Bedwin the Bishop and Gwarthegydd son of Caw and a young man. Iddawg brought Rhonabwy and his friends to the king, who immediately asked the Stirrer where he got these little men. As Iddawg explained that he had found them on the road, Arthur smirked. Iddawg wanted to know what the joke was. Arthur replied that he hadn't been laughing – he was just appalled to see that such wretched men as these were guarding this island after the good men who used to guard it. Iddawg pointed out to Rhonabwy that the king was wearing a ring with a special stone in it that would enable the dreamer who saw it to remember everything that he had seen.

Two armies came to the ford. The leader of the second one (Addaon, son of Taliesin) spurred his stallion through the ford and in doing so splashed Arthur and the bishop, who were left as wet as if they had just been pulled out of the river. The young man standing by Arthur (Elffin, son of Gwyddno) struck the offending horse with his sword and had a brief argument with its rider. Then Caradog Freichfras, Arthur's cousin and chief adviser, pointed out that the enormous army which was gathered in such a confined space had promised to be at the battle of Baddon by midday, fighting against Osla Gyllellfawr.

This remark is a sign that the dream (like most dreams) has its own peculiar chronology. The battle of Baddon or Badon Hill or Mons Badonicus was supposed to have been the greatest of Arthur's victories. It was said to have taken place at the end of the fifth or the beginning of the sixth century. The final battle of Arthur's career was the disastrous encounter with his nephew Medrawd at Camlan, described by the *Trioedd Ynys Prydein* ('Triads of the Island of Britain') as one of the 'three futile battles of the Island of Britain'. According to the *Annales Cambriae* the battle of Camlan took place twenty one years after the victory of Badon Hill.[9] In Rhonabwy's dream, however, Camlan has already taken place at least seven years before, while Baddon/Badon Hill is just about to happen.

Melville Richards, in his edition of the story, assumed that the author was following Geoffrey of Monmouth by identifying Caer Faddon with Bath.[10] My own feeling, given the highly localised setting of the story, is that the author made a link between Baddon and Buttington (on the far side of Rhyd-y-groes-ar-Hafren). He would then have used Caer Faddon as another name for Caer Digoll, the hillfort on the Long Mountain or Cefn Digoll (the 'Unlost Hillside'). The story refers to the armies setting off through the ford in that direction. The enemy whom

Arthur is to confront there is another anachronism. Osla Gyllellfawr ('Osla Bigknife') is Offa, the eighth-century king of Mercia. Offa's Dyke runs through Buttington, which suggests that the 'Unlost Hillside' may actually have been lost for a short time before being won back by the Powysmen.[11]

Rhonabwy noticed two armies, one in white and the other in black, coming towards the ford. Iddawg explained that one was the Norsemen and the other was the Danes. Then Eiryn Wych Amheibyn, Arthur's ugly servant, stretched out a magic cloak and put a huge chair on it and Arthur sat down on it and challenged Owain son of Urien to a game of *gwyddbwyll*. This is the word used for chess in modern Welsh. The medieval version played by the two heroes involved golden pieces (described as *'gwerin'* or 'ordinary folk') on a silver board.[12] The players were engrossed in their game when they were interrupted by a curly-headed young squire (described in great detail), who reported that Arthur's young servants and squires were upsetting Owain's ravens and asked him to get the emperor to intervene. Owain made the request. Arthur's response was curt: ' *"Gware dy chware", heb ef'* ('"Play your game,"' he said').

They continued to play. Another elaborately dressed squire arrived with a report that the emperor's squires were troubling Owain's ravens and wounding and even killing some of them. Owain asked Arthur a second time to stop his men from attacking the ravens. Arthur replied: *'Gware dy chware'*. The game continued. Then a third, furiously angry squire (again with elaborate accoutrements) galloped over to tell Owain that his most special crows had been killed and that the others were so badly hurt and wounded that they could no longer fly higher than six feet from the earth. After Arthur had ignored a third plea from Owain, the prince told his squire to wave his flag in the place where the fighting was at its worst and what God desired would be done.

As the squire raised the flag the weary birds recovered their strength and became aggressive and confident, flying down and attacking Arthur's men. The noise of the crows' exultant cawing and beating of wings and the screams of the men whom they were wounding and killing was such that even Owain and Arthur could hear it as they sat playing their game. A knight rode up to tell Arthur what the crows were doing to his men. The emperor told the prince to call his birds off. This time it was

Owain's turn to respond with '*Gware dy chware*'. And the game went on. By now the crows had begun to lift Arthur's men into the air, tearing them apart and letting the bits fall back to the ground.

A second knight rode up to report the disastrous consequences of what was happening. He said that so many squires and young servants and sons of the noblemen of the Island of Britain were being killed that it would be difficult to defend the island from then onwards. Owain still wouldn't stop his birds and insisted that the game went on.

The crows were now picking up weapons and horses as well as men and dropping them to the earth. The weapons remained whole, but the animals and people were torn to pieces. A third knight rode over to say that Arthur's escort and the sons of the nobility of the island had been killed. Then Arthur commanded Owain to call off the ravens, and this time picked up the pieces from the board and squeezed them until they turned to dust. Owain's flag was lowered and peace returned. Rhonabwy asked Iddawg the names of the squires and the knights. Interestingly the first name in the list was that of one of the most unfortunate figures in the early history of Powys: Selyf son of Cynan Garwyn, the Cadelling prince who died at the battle of Chester.

Twenty-four knights arrived from Osla Gyllellfawr to arrange a peace with Arthur. Arthur called his council together (the impressive list of names reveals the author's familiarity with characters from traditional Welsh storytelling). Then the poets came to sing Arthur's praises. And apart from one wise young man no one could understand their poem, except that they knew that it was in praise of Arthur. Then twenty-four asses laden with gold and silver appeared, sent from Greece as tribute to Arthur. He gave both the animals and their burden to the poets as a reward. Peace was declared – and Rhonabwy woke up. He had been sleeping on the yellow heifer's skin for three days and three nights. The author ends the tale by saying that no poet or storyteller will be able to repeat it without a book because of all the detailed descriptions that it contains.

Breuddwyd Rhonabwy is a sending up of the heroic tradition that had played such an important part in the dreams and aspirations of Powys for so many centuries. The contrast between the 'little men', Rhonabwy and his companions, and the giant figures who appear in the dream may seem to suggest at first that the great heroes of the past have been succeeded by feeble pygmies in the present (as Arthur himself implies). The contrast between the squalor of Heilyn's flea-ridden farmhouse and the splendour of the tents and the dress of the squires and knights at Rhyd-y-groes-ar-Hafren apparently reinforces that message.

Arthur and Owain are two of the greatest figures in the Welsh heroic tradition. The traditions linked to Arthur are discussed at length elsewhere.[13] The lament that the historical Taliesin, the first major poet from Powys, wrote for his patron, Owain ab Urien, is one of the masterpieces of the earliest Welsh literature:

> May the Lord consider heaven necessary
> For the soul of Owain son of Urien.
> It was not hard to sing for
> The ruler of the green land of Rheged.
> Deserving of praise he lies in a grave:
> His dawn-winged spear was fiery!
> There will never be anyone equal
> To the lord of bright Llwyfenydd;
> Reaper of enemies, with a powerful grip,
> And the same bold nature as his father and grandfather.
> When Owain killed Fflamddwyn
> He could have done it in his sleep!
> The broad hosts of England sleep
> With light in their eyes.
> And those who didn't retreat a little
> Were braver than they needed to be.
> Owain punished them angrily
> Like a wolf attacking sheep.
> A splendid man, with many-coloured armour,
> Who gave stallions to supplicants.
> He gathered wealth like a miser:
> He shared it for his soul's sake:
> The soul of Owain son of Urien.[14]

By the time that *Breuddwyd Rhonabwy* was composed Owain ab Urien had become associated with the Arthurian myth. He is the central figure in a Welsh Arthurian romance that has been dated to the early twelfth century.[15]

There is nothing heroic about Owain or Arthur in Rhonabwy's dream. They are supposed to be going off together to win Arthur's greatest victory. Instead they linger by the river wasting time with a board game. Even the terrible suffering of their followers scarcely distracts them from their playing. In the end peace breaks out without a battle having taken place between them and their Mercian enemy. The bards sing Arthur's praises in meaningless praise-sounding phrases that deliver a sarcastic sideswipe at the deliberately obscure vocabulary of the poets of the princes. They are richly rewarded for extolling an emperor who has done nothing in a song that only one person understands. This is a satire on Powys's view of its past as well as the miserable state of its present.

Helen Fulton has recently given a reading of the story in which she identifies its portrayal of Arthur as a depiction of Llywelyn ap Iorwerth. She sees him as being presented as an ineffectual national leader, who had usurped the place formerly held by the more successful rulers of individual kingdoms such as Madog ap Maredudd and Owain Gwynedd. She suggests that the Owain in the story might remind the audience of Madog and even contain a prophecy that Llywelyn's supremacy might be overcome.[16] The idea that Arthur represents Llywelyn is certainly an attractive one. I am not quite so sure about the other details of her theory. The story certainly contains a considerable element of contemporary political comment, but its central thrust is, to my mind, a critique of the inflated and unrealistic heroic ideals which had become the staple of so much of the poetry written in praise of Welsh princes. Such ideals seemed to have been revealed as an empty sham by the death of Gwenwynwyn and the disappearance of Powys.

No doubt there was laughter when the author first read out *Breuddwyd Rhonabwy* – but behind the humour the storyteller's artistry must have left his audience with a devastating sense of emptiness. Admittedly there had always been a certain ambiguity about Powys's attitude towards heroism. The traditions about Tysilio and the poetry describing Llywarch Hen's argument with his youngest son are evidence of this. However no one had previously gone so far as the border storyteller did. Rhonabwy's dream suggested that there were no more heroes – and that perhaps there never had been any.

ii) The Last Hero?

The career of Gruffudd ap Gwenwynwyn might seem to confirm the
cynical attitude towards the heroic expressed by the author of *Breuddwyd
Rhonabwy*. Gruffudd was certainly no hero and he is usually listed among
the villains of Welsh history. This was not entirely his own fault. He had
spent twenty-five years as an exile in England. During that time he had
been totally dependent on the crumbs from the king of England's table
and the kindness of his mother's family, the Corbets of Caus Castle in
Shropshire.[17] When he was restored as lord of his father's lands in 1241, it
was as a feudal vassal of Henry III. Like Gwenwynwyn before him,
Gruffudd was to be caught between the rulers of Gwynedd and the
English king. His attempts to become a free agent failed. He was about as
independent as one of the pieces on Arthur and Urien's *gwyddbwyll* board
as the two heroes 'played their game'.

In 1244 Dafydd ap Llywelyn of Gwynedd attacked Gruffudd, who
had refused to join an alliance against King Henry. The lord of Powys
Wenwynwyn was forced to swear allegiance to the ruler of Gwynedd.
However his true loyalty remained to the English king. As a result he was
attacked early in 1257 by Llywelyn ap Gruffudd and some other
powerful Welsh leaders and lost almost all his land. All that remained to
him was Welshpool castle, some of the valley of the river Severn and a
small area of Caereinion. Later in the year Llywelyn renewed his assault
and Gruffudd lost everything. He was forced into exile again. By 1263
the English king had become embroiled in domestic troubles as Simon
de Montfort and his barons rose up against him. Gruffudd saw
compromise with Llywelyn as his only hope.

He therefore sacrificed his claim to part of his territory and swore
allegiance to the ruler of Gwynedd as part of the latter's plan to make
himself prince of Wales.[18]

In 1274 Gruffudd and his son, Owain, were involved in a plot against
Llywelyn. Llywelyn responded by seizing part of Gruffudd's territory and
taking Owain prisoner. Towards the end of the year Gruffudd imprisoned
some of Llywelyn's messengers. In response Llywelyn captured Welshpool
castle and completely destroyed it. Gruffudd was forced into exile again,
this time in Shrewsbury, and Llywelyn annexed all his territory.[19] In 1276
Gruffudd regained some of his lands with the assistance of Edward I and

the following year the English king forced Llywelyn to release Owain ap Gruffudd ap Gwenwynwyn. Gruffudd gave Edward his support in the final campaign against Llywelyn.[20] This has led many Welsh writers to depict Gwenwynwyn's son as a villainous traitor. However Professor Rhys Davies has recently given a much more balanced view of the position of Powys and its leaders:

> Powys stood in the way of the unification of native Wales; its rulers, particularly those of southern Powys, preferred to submit to the king of England rather than subsume their ambitions in the vision of a united Wales ruled by the house of Gwynedd . . . There was no reason why the princelings of Powys should find the status of being 'Welsh barons' of the prince of Wales more acceptable than that of being tenants-in-chief of the king of England. Indeed, a distant suzerain might be preferable and less exacting than a neighbouring prince. Powys's achievement was to have survived and to have adjusted its ambitions to accord more closely with the realities of power. Dependence was the price of survival; the alternative was extinction. Gruffudd ap Gwenwynwyn of southern Powys could congratulate himself, as he lay dying in 1286, that he, his dynasty, and his patrimonial inheritance had survived, while the other two major principalities and dynasties of native Wales had been extinguished (or virtually so).
>
> R. R. Davies, *The Age of Conquest: Wales 1063-1415* (Oxford, 1991), p. 236. Reprinted by permission of Oxford University Press.

Political realism is rarely heroic.

From 1286 onwards the lords of Powys Wenwynwyn were effectively Marcher barons, aping their Anglo-Norman counterparts. Owain ap Gruffudd ap Gwenwynwyn changed his name to Owen de la Pole. On the death of his son Gruffudd in 1309, the lands went to his sister's husband, John de Cherleton.[21] The latter was strongly opposed to attempts to revive any form of Welsh independence. He took action against Welsh rebels in 1316 and by the late 1320s had become convinced that Ystrad Marchell with its Welsh monks had become a hotbed of sedition. De Cherleton persuaded King Edward III to get the abbot of Clairvaux to set up an inquiry into the state of affairs in the abbey on the banks of the Severn. The Welsh monks and abbot were to be thrown out and replaced by Englishmen. The local magnate also wanted to sever the links between Ystrad Marchell and its founding house at Whitland. Its new visitor was to be the abbot of Buildwas in Shropshire.[22]

What may have been the true reason for the action against Ystrad Marchell emerged in one of Edward's letters which referred to 'unlawful assemblies to excite contention and hatred between the English and the Welsh' taking place at the abbey.[23] Apparently the replacement monks were still unacceptable to de Cherleton. In 1333 the newly-elected abbot, Matthew, and the commissary of the abbot of Clairvaux both petitioned the king to say that de Cherleton's soldiers were preventing the monks and abbot from holding services in their abbey. The lord of Powys had gone so far as to threaten the commissary with injury or death. The king intervened, ordering de Cherleton to allow the monks access to their abbey. De Cherleton was alleged to have said 'I am Pope, I am King, and Bishop and Abbot in my land.'[24] The Welsh abbot who was apparently expelled by John de Cherleton was a certain Gruffudd. He is mentioned sympathetically by John's grandson, also called John de Cherleton, in a charter of 1367.[25] It is perhaps not surprising that when a new Welsh hero emerged in the borderland at the end of the fourteenth century, his opponents included John de Cherleton's great-grandsons, John and Edward.[26]

Owain Glyndŵr was lord of Glyndyfrdwy in the valley of the river Dee between Llangollen and Corwen and Cynllaith Owain, a fertile area near the English border. His chief residence was in this second lordship at Sycharth in the parish of Llansilin. Owain was a direct descendant of Madog ap Maredudd, the last prince of a united Powys. He was born either 1354 or 1359 and educated at the Inns of Court in London. He then became a squire, fighting in the service of the English nobility. In 1387 he was one of the 127 esquires in the retinue of the earl of Arundel. He took part in Richard II's wars in Scotland and may also have served the king in France and Ireland as well.[27]

Owain became a patron of Iolo Goch, a native of the Vale of Clwyd, who is generally regarded as the most important Welsh poet of the second half of the fourteenth century. Iolo wrote a poem tracing Owain's ancestry, another in praise of his courage, and a third containing a wonderful description of his court at Sycharth.[28] Gruffydd Aled Williams has recently identified a fourth poem written by Iolo in praise of the lord of Glyndyfrdwy. He dates its composition as sometime between 1401 and 1403, when Owain's rebellion was at the height of its success and the aged poet could rejoice in his hero's triumph over English arrogance.[29]

Owain's earlier martial feats had also caught the attention and imagination of one of the most gifted poets of Powys Wenwynwyn, Gruffudd Llwyd ab Einion Llygliw, a native of Llangadfan. Gruffudd Llwyd, like Iolo Goch, belonged to the new breed of poets that had emerged after the demise of the courts of the princes: poets who now depended on the patronage of the *uchelwyr* (gentry) for their survival. In a poem to Hywel ap Meurig Fychan of Nannau and his brother Meurig Llwyd, Gruffudd justified his craft:

> O God, is it a sin for man
> To receive yellow gold for a song of praise?
> Praising is a blessed employment, as good as the payment,
> If God doesn't punish those who do it.
> Is it lawful to accept payment from a generous person?
> Lawful and not sinful if it is given.
> The *Elucidarium*, a faulty work,
> Told me that on two counts
> Praising in song and selling a poem of praise
> Was a cause of my great weight of sin.
> Shame on his powerful judgement,
> Besides I don't want him as a teacher,
> Because I don't know (which is a worry),
> Who the author that wrote this was.
> Why should he insult us from afar,
> If he can't help us?
> In answering the accusation I won't despair,
> I'm not one of the lowest class of worthless, untrained poets:
> I'm not a wandering entertainer with loose morals.
> No – I know how to shape a proper poem.
> Nor am I, though I am a poet,
> A rhymester from the fairs, a shameful service.
> The Holy Spirit, whose praise is flawless,
> Gives me a poetic gift that grows in me.
> He, my excellent treasure, will put a stop
> To the accusation of falsehood against his poet.[30]

Gruffudd Llwyd combined wit and versatility. Not only did he praise the gentry, he also wrote some entertaining love poems, two major religious poems (which we will come to later) and a deservedly famous *cywydd* which has become known as '*I'r haul ac i Forgannwg*' ('To the sun and to

Glamorgan').[31] His two poems to Owain Glyndŵr make it clear that in the lord of Sycharth and Glyndyfrdwy he felt that he had come across the sort of hero that the poets of Powys had been longing for ever since the days of Cynddelw and Owain Cyfeiliog.

It was perhaps inevitable that Gruffudd should feel compelled to compare Owain Glyndŵr with another Owain: the hero who was the subject of Taliesin's lament and who was rather less flatteringly portrayed playing *gwyddbwyll* in Rhonabwy's dream.[32] In describing Owain Glyndŵr's exploits in Scotland, Gruffudd deliberately refers to an incident from *Iarlles y Ffynnon* ('The Lady of the Fountain'). In this Arthurian romance, Owain son of Urien is a member of Arthur's court who goes on a quest that involves successfully vanquishing a black knight by a fountain with a deadly spear-thrust. The knight had previously defeated Cynon, another of Arthur's followers.[33] He also compares Owain with a famous Norman knight of the borderland: Fulke Fitzwarine ('Ffwg' in Welsh), who had once been Owain Cyfeiliog's opponent. Gruffudd writes:

> You travelled, you journeyed in pursuit,
> Like wonderful Owain ab Urien in former times,
> When he was the swift piercer
> Of the black knight of the water;
> He was a hero when he struck,
> Chief fighter of the far fountain . . .
> You, Owain, had an easy journey,
> You cut, lord, a terrible path with your sword.
> Praiseworthy baron, you'll be counted a friend
> Of tall Urien's son, doing the same deed
> As when he, with his deep-piercing spear,
> Came face to face with the fountain's chief knight.
> Kind, dear one, terrible in battle,
> Another Fulke for bravery,
> When your work was at its hardest
> Fighting the wall of soldiers
> Your steel-tipped spear shattered in your hand,
> Cruel torch, into three pieces.
> Everyone saw in your lovely hand,
> In the praiseworthy attack, your spear like a sparking fire,
> As you smote the battlefield you broke

Your spear almost down to your fist.
Through power and furiousness of heart
And strength of arm, shoulder and breast
You caused, my lord, through your terrible work
Flashing columns between the wood and the steel;
Then, a fortunate foray, with the force of hired oxen
You pursued, great gifted lord, the army –
In twos and threes that great crowd was all scattered.[34]

Owain's exploits made him, in Gruffudd Llwyd's eyes, a natural leader at a time when Wales was in a state of acute depression and despair. In a second poem, the poet describes the wretchedness of the country and its people:

The Welsh are so oppressed that they've become
A society of wretches like drunken crows:
I could, as I don't want to make a profit,
Describe them as a cauldron for boiling offal.
Those with least gentility
Have highest status, it makes me sigh,
And the politest before midday
Will be most despised and diffident.[35]

Gruffudd Llwyd then lists some of the ancient heroes of the past and goes on to think of a contemporary who fits into the same pattern. He asks who can fulfil this position, and answers:

Owain, Lord of Glyndyfrdwy, a narrow valley, remains,
I know of no more excellent Lord;
A young, gifted nobleman from a generous feast-giving lineage
Of Sycharth, a gathering place for battle . . .[36]

The battle began in 1400. Its most probable catalyst was a dispute between Owain and his neighbour, Lord Grey of Rhuthun.[37] The campaign developed over the following years. A victory at Mynydd Hyddgen in 1401 helped to broaden Owain's support and the next year he vanquished a large English force at Bryn Glas (Pilleth). King Henry IV then managed to defeat some of Owain's English allies, led by Henry Percy ('Hotspur'), the Earl of Northumberland's son, at the battle of Shrewsbury. Nevertheless Owain Glyndŵr's grip on Wales was

strengthened as castle after castle fell into his hands. In 1404 he captured
the key strongholds of Aberystwyth and Harlech and signed a treaty with
the French. Owain was now styling himself 'prince of Wales, by the grace
of God'. In 1405 he made an agreement with Edmund Mortimer and
the Earl of Northumberland which (if it had ever been more than
wishful thinking on the part of all three of them) would have given him
a substantial area of England as well as the whole of Wales.

However the English now started to hit back. First Owain's followers
were defeated at Grosmont. Then his son was captured and his brother
killed in a disastrous engagement at Pwll Melyn, near Usk. Owain
summoned a Welsh parliament at Harlech (he had held an earlier one in
Machynlleth the year before). He hoped that it would help to provide
him with money and men for a counterattack. His French allies landed at
Milford Haven and the joint army captured Haverfordwest and Carmarthen.
Rhys Davies has recently cast doubt on the old tradition that the combined
force then crossed the English border and almost reached Worcester
before turning back.[38] Owain began negotiating with the Antipope Benedict
XIII of Avignon. His dream was to make the Church in Wales independent
of Canterbury, with an archbishop of St Davids who would control
several English dioceses as well as the Welsh ones. All clergy in Wales
were to be Welsh-speaking and Welsh universities were to be established.

The tide of Owain's fortunes gradually began to ebb. In 1408 the
English recaptured Aberystwyth and a few months later Harlech fell. The
Welsh prince's wife, daughters and granddaughters were captured there
and he lost the centre from which he had been able to rule with all the
trappings of a head of state. Guerrilla warfare continued. A last major raid
on the Shropshire border was defeated in 1410. Two years later one of
Owain's leading opponents, Dafydd Gam, was captured by Glyndŵr's
men and a ransom had to be paid for his release. The rebellion slowly
faded away. Owain himself disappeared from view. He possibly spent his
declining years incognito at his daughter's home in Herefordshire.[39]

One of Owain's supporters during the closing phase of the revolt was
a young poet from Powys Wenwynwyn. Llywelyn ab y Moel came from
Llanwnnog in Arwystli but he also had connections with the borderland.
His mother came from Meifod and he had relations in the Llanymynech
area. After his death Llywelyn was described as 'Owain's song-thrush'.[40]
One of his early poems, describing the naked trees of a birch grove in

winter, calls them 'the spears of Owain's best men'.[41] Llywelyn was one of a group of Owain's followers who were defeated in a battle at Waun Gaseg (possibly near Abbey Cwm-hir in Radnorshire).

> It was painful to see, I'm a witness,
> At Waun Gaseg, spears left unused,
> The anguish of our men in the grass . . .[42]

Because of his part in the rebellion, the poet had to take refuge in one of the wild places along the border. These became the haunts of outlaws who had once served with Glyndŵr. Llywelyn's hideout was in the woods of Y Graig Lwyd (now known as the White Rock) at Llanymynech, probably because he had relatives nearby. He describes it as being a veritable city swarming with outlawed rebels:

> A broad sky above the hiding place,
> You are the London of Owain's people,
> A grove of trees full of outlaws,
> Broader than the field of the moon or seas.[43]

From there, he tells us, he would slip over to raid Ruyton XI Towns a few miles to the east. This small Shropshire borough belonged to the Fitzalan family, who were zealous supporters of the English king and therefore regarded as fair game.[44] Even Llanymynech became too dangerous in the end, and he had to disappear towards Radnorshire in the hope of finding a safer hiding place.

Llywelyn ab y Moel died in 1440 and (unlike Cynddelw) does not seem to have had any trouble in persuading the monks of Ystrad Marchell to bury him in their abbey on the banks of the river Severn a few miles south of the rock where he had once hidden. This has led some writers to speculate that the poet might possibly have become a monk in his later years. Guto'r Glyn, one of his most distinguished contemporaries, lamented:

> There's a coffin in Ystrad Marchell
> In the graveyard of the monks and their cells . . .
> Where Llywelyn was put
> By work of hand and spade – a place to weep . . .
> And Owain's song-thrush is silenced,
> A mute man in oak and stone.[45]

iii) Visions of God

If Gruffudd Llwyd had been one of Owain Glyndŵr's greatest admirers, Llywelyn ab y Moel, Owain's ex-soldier, had an equally profound admiration for Gruffudd Llwyd. In a poetic argument with Rhys Goch Eryri, the erstwhile outlaw praised Gruffudd as a religious poet:

> He was a poet to the Father on his throne,
> He was a poet, a poet to Mary;
> He was a poet to the sacrificed Son,
> He was a poet to the Spirit rightly together with them . . .[46]

Two of Gruffudd Llwyd's religious poems survive. The first is a poem to God that stresses his role as the source of everything that is. Gruffudd begins by intertwining the persons of the Trinity to express their relationship:

> Great Creator, pure kind Maker,
> Christ the treasure, Mary the Virgin's son,
> Lord, only Son of God the Ruler,
> Listen to me, generous three-personed God,
> Father, Spirit as one Lord,
> And true Son from Mary the Virgin's womb.
> You are Spirit, your heart pierced through,
> And God as well as man, I greet you all![47]

He then outlines his view of humanity's place in God's creation:

> True God, you directed towards man
> Endless love without measure.
> You created man rather than any other creature,
> You suffered anguish
> To sustain us eternally,
> You saved and won humankind,
> In your own image to worship you,
> The guardians of other creatures;
> Their reward will be great if they deserve it,
> They are all as man desires.
> Every stallion and every ox ploughs
> And turns the land, true great God:
> From thence comes bread for man
> If he works;

A shoal of fish from the ocean
Comes to man, to whom belongs blessing;
Certainly every bird
Learns to honour man:
Wild birds on their high paths,
Hawks as fast as the wind,
Wild creatures lie down for man
And come tamely onto his hand.
Your splendid miracles are magnificent
Within plants and stones;
Because of your skilful work, Mary's Son,
Fire can be had from stone;
You caused new oil and wine
To come from wood;
It's certain that a crwth or harp
Try to tame man's anger.
It would be fair for us to thank you,
Good beautiful God, for your goodness.[48]

However, despite the wonder of creation and humanity's privileged position within it, the poet believes that we still treat God with contempt:

In deep faith, no other creature
Of those that you've made
Does so much to make you an enemy,
As man does – you know what pain is,
Passion causing hurt.
Men swear by your body, your flesh,
And your wonderful image as though they have faith;
Others, to humiliate you utterly,
Swear by the blood of your wounded breast.
You should be worshipped completely, but often
Your five wounds are insulted.
Note the refusal, a sad man should never take
God's name in vain.[49]

Man's thoughtless attitude towards God is compounded by the way in which he behaves towards his fellow human beings. An element of social criticism creeps in as Gruffudd condemns the way in which powerful magnates extort money from the poor and helpless in order to use it to curry favour with the king. He suggests that such behaviour could have apocalyptic consequences:

> Why also in the world will each man be
> Another's enemy?
> The world is ugly in unfortunate sorrow,
> Holding office won't let you sleep for a night.
> Powerful men generously give
> Gold to their ruler, for far-reaching praise,
> And promise it although that angers the people,
> Collecting it from the weak.
> In wise faithfulness, no one should give,
> In spite of pain, gold at another's cost;
> Dignity is now a short-lived drunken honour,
> A wastefulness, if a generous prodigal
> Wants to give away extravagantly, let's be agreed,
> He should do so from his own wealth.
> It's a cruel song if he doesn't do that:
> The great sea shatters the land's defences,
> Lightning destroys the forests with fire
> And wind uproots the trees.
> Before this happens, and complaints are expressed,
> Check out and discover the truth.[50]

The end of all things is the Day of Judgement. Gruffudd Llwyd's description of it is based on Jesus' parable of the sheep and the goats (Matthew 25.31–46). However the vivid nature in which he portrays it suggests that it may be inspired (like his other religious poem) by a painting or a carving that he has seen in a church.

> Every day we are getting nearer
> The end of a good life,
> And some day we'll receive an official call
> Because we've followed the wrong path,
> So that there will not be (a mild phrase)
> A hindrance to beautiful holiness.
> The earth (that's been properly prepared)
> Shall quake and the trees shall wither;
> Men or trees bearing fruit shall only exceptionally
> Be found innocent.
> When, in spite of our opposition,

The Day of Judgment's Trumpet sounds and the dear host
Come to take us, as if in an hour,
That day to the one great mountain,
There, you, Christ, shall be, worthy of glory,
A blessing to the Christian world,
Displaying from your court of judgement
Your wounds to the hosts,
Welcoming a blessed crowd, in your presence,
To your right hand, a fortunate declaration,
And the unbelievers shall go at once
To your left hand because of what they have done;
A terrible experience, the punishment is very severe
For the man with judgement on his forehead.
A pity for those who did not deserve your protection, Lord,
A splendid blessing, through justice;
Blessed the faithful, sinless one!
Pity the body that's very guilty! [51]

Gruffudd Llwyd's poem to God reflects a degree of gloom that was not uncharacteristic of late fourteenth-century Western Europe as the traumatic results of the Black Death continued to cast a long shadow. This pessimism would deepen in Wales in the period after the collapse of Glyndŵr's rebellion and its bleakness would find expression in the extraordinary poetry of Siôn Cent.

Llwyd's other religious poem is brighter in tone. A song of praise to the Trinity, it was inspired by an image in the parish church of St Mary of the Salutation, Welshpool. St Mary's dates from the mid-thirteenth century, but was substantially rebuilt during the following hundred years. [52] The dedication of the church probably influenced the beginning of the poem. It starts with a declaration of the poet's faith, followed by a typical medieval description of the way in which the Holy Spirit came to Mary:

I believe with a sincere faith
In God the Father, whom no deceit can reach,
And in the Holy Spirit, Lord together with him,
And in the Son, as Mary knows,
He is One, it is right to declare him
The Lord of teachers, and Three.
The Father was before memory,

Because of his blessing
I accept his grace.
We frequently hear, if we believe,
That he is the Holy Spirit as well
Who came before anyone
From God's mouth and countenance.
When the Spirit came from heaven, a vocal cry,
In the form of a white humble bird,
The speech in the ear of a beautiful maiden
Mattered, a gentle splendour.
Then he went, because of his grace,
The One in heaven and the just Three,
To endure war with the enemy,
True God and humble man.[53]

The poet then decides to penetrate deeper into the mystery of the Trinity, using the image of a stag's three horns and a hart's single horn; the roots, trunk and branches of a tree; and the rays of the sun shining through glass:

This poem is a perfect and fitting song of praise:
Some do not know who the Trinity is;
I know, his love belongs to me,
If I did not know that, the pain would not leave me:
The stag can carry
The branches of his horns, a finely wrought ladder
On a dignified forehead, my support,
They grow lovely and splendid;
Three privileged branches, a fortunate right,
Before he is six months old,
And one pointed horn, an excellent development,
Are always on a hart's head.
So in the same way, a gift of praise,
The lovely yew is like the only God:
The green tree has a root,
And a strong body, and branches,
And it is a sincere gift of love,
One tree that reaches up to heaven.
The lovely partition of glorious light
Appears wonderful to me.
Through a smooth wall of glass, excellently and generously arranged,

Shine the sun's long rays;
And the glass and the sphere
Are completely united. [54]

Gruffudd Llwyd examines the mystery of the Incarnation, where God is born as man through the Holy Spirit and the Virgin Mary:

It was easier than this for the only God
To send his generous Spirit
To Mary, to the heart of a slender, shapely, beautiful body,
Like sending a son to be fostered.
Gabriel, an acknowledged angel,
Following the command of the God of heaven,
Sent the gentle Word to Mary
And the Word became Mary's son:
And the Word was easy to love,
And the Word was Mary's Son:
A Word from heaven became our friend,
Truly he was ours, God overcame.
As the beginning of John's Gospel says
In a beautiful way of holy God,
The Word existed from the beginning,
And God was the Word, whose love lasts long.
It's right to call him, an excellent expression,
Three and One as church law says.
Then immediately a crown from heaven
Was presented for our beloved,
A sign of God's approval, because there was,
Despite his wounded breast, no other king but him.[55]

Gruffudd Llwyd then turns to the image of the Trinity in the church at Welshpool that has inspired his poem:

A good intention, gorgeous wealth,
We bow low before his naked image.
His image is visible there in the church,
On a beautiful Sunday, splendidly praised,
Just as he is, pity the doubters,
Christ my love is in the chancel
At Welshpool, worthy is the Father
And the Son who brings great peace

And the Holy Spirit with him;
At night to show his excellence
Inside his dwelling place, there's light;
In daytime through the blessed hours,
There are people and splendid bells,
Brothers who chant of paradise,
A lovely choir and beautiful candles.
Why does the organ sound daily
To the joy of the host of believers?
For the sake of the Son and his sacrifice,
And the Father and the Spirit in powerful union,
As says the gleaming cry
Of the Psalm's shining title: *Laudate*.[56]

The poem ends with a hymn of praise which emphasises that everything that exists depends on God:

Choir instruments, fair strings,
Praise him through frequent phrases,
And the stars and the heavenly host,
And the sea and the earth praise him,
And fish from the waters obey the command,
They praise their Lord.
Seahorses praise him
As they are ordered;
Man's tongue is useless
To sing poetry with excitement
Unless he praises, an excellent prayer,
His most greatly loved one who was on the cross.
In the age of the Spirit, there was not, is not,
Will not be anything without the Lord.
I know that I can strive for nothing
Without him, generous God and Son,
There'll be no right and true poem in me,
No body, no soul, no reason,
No change of mind, no moving feet,
Or turning of the eye or hand,
No throne of heaven, no refuge,
No earth, nothing tame or wild,
No second of existence, no life,
Nor is there anything for us without him.[57]

Gruffudd Llwyd's two great religious poems represent a final pre-Reformation flowering of the spiritual tradition of the borderland. That tradition was certainly not at an end. It would flower again in the *Plygain* carols and, most remarkably, in the hymns of Ann Griffiths, Dolwar Fach, at the beginning of the nineteenth century.

As we have seen throughout this study, the tension between heroism and holiness was a characteristic of the culture of the Powys borderland for a thousand years. This conflict could at times produce some savage ironies. Perhaps one of the cruellest of them comes near the end of the story. On the one hand, Gruffudd Llwyd had identified Owain Glyndŵr as a new hero in the lineage of the great heroes of the past: a potential redeemer for Powys and Wales. On the other, Gruffudd Llwyd's religious masterpiece, his great poem to the Trinity, had been inspired by an image or painting in St Mary's Church in Welshpool. The chronicler Adam of Usk recorded that, in the autumn of 1401, that same church was despoiled by the supporters of Owain Glyndŵr. It seems certain that they destroyed the source of the poet's inspiration during their rampage.[58]

NOTES

[1] Richards, *Breudwyt*, pp.xxxvii–xxxix.

[2] A suggestion that the story is a satire on Llywelyn ap Iorwerth, written after his seizure of Powys from Gwenwynwyn in 1216, has recently been made by Helen Fulton, 'Cyd-destun Gwleidyddol *Breudwyt Rhonabwy*', *Llên Cymru* XXII (1999), 42-56.

[3] Enid Roberts, *Braslun o Hanes Llên Powys* (Denbigh, 1965), p.42.

[4] Thomas, *Charters*, pp.3, 201-2.

[5] Rhiannon Ifans, *Gwerthfawrogi'r Chwedlau* (Aberystwyth, 1999), p.216.

[6] *Gwaith Cynddelw Brydydd Mawr*, I, 143-53.

[7] Richards, *Breudwyt*, pp.29-30.

[8] Richards, *Breudwyt*, pp.37-8.

[9] Bromwich, *Trioedd*, p.206; Nennius, *History and Annals*, pp.45,85.

[10] Richards, *Breudwyt*, p.46.

[11] T.I. Ellis, *Crwydro Maldwyn* (Llandybie, 1957), p.74; Helen Burnham, *A Guide to Ancient and Historic Wales: Clwyd and Powys* (London, 1995), p.112.

[12] Richards, *Breudwyt*, pp.50-1.

[13] See *The Arthur of the Welsh: The Arthurian Legend in Medieval Welsh Literature*, edited by Rachel Bromwich, A.O.H. Jarman and Brynley F. Roberts (Cardiff, 1991)

[14] Williams, *Canu Taliesin*, p.12.

[15] *Owein or Chwedyl Iarlles y Ffynnawn*, edited by R.L.Thomson (Dublin, 1975), p.xxi.

[16] Fulton, 'Cyd-destun Gwleidyddol *Breudwyt Rhonabwy*', p.55.

[17] *Dictionary of Welsh Biography*, pp.316-17 ('Gruffydd ap Gwenwynwyn').

[18] *Brut*, pp.106, 110-1; J. Beverley Smith, *Llywelyn ap Gruffudd, Tywysog Cymru* (Cardiff, 1986),pp.134-8.

[19] *Brut*, pp.116-7; Smith, *Llywelyn ap Gruffudd*, pp.259-68.

[20] *Brut*, pp.118-20.

[21] *Dictionary of Welsh Biography*, pp.316-17 ('Gruffydd ap Gwenwynwyn'), p.74 ('Cherleton or Charlton family'); R.R. Davies, *Lordship and Society in the March of Wales 1282-1400* (Oxford, 1978), pp.49, 286-7.

[22] Morris Charles Jones, 'The Abbey of Ystrad Marchell (Strata Marcella) or Pola', *Montgomeryshire Collections*, V (1872), 109-48 (pp. 138-47);Thomas, *Charters*, 31-2.

[23] Williams, *Welsh Cistercians*, I, 56.

[24] Williams, *Welsh Cistercians*, I, 56-7;Thomas, *Charters*, 32-3.

[25] Thomas, *Charters*, pp.228-30.

[26] *Dictionary of Welsh Biography*, p.74 ('Cherleton or Charlton family').

[27] For Owain Glyndŵr see J.E. Lloyd, *Owen Glendower* (Felinfach, 1992); Glanmor Williams, *Owen Glendower* (Oxford, 1966); R.R. Davies, *The Revolt of Owain Glyndŵr* (Oxford, 1995); Elissa R. Henken, *National Redeemer: Owain Glyndŵr in Welsh Tradition* (Cardiff, 1996).

[28] *Gwaith Iolo Goch*, edited by D.R. Johnston (Cardiff, 1988), pp.36-50. For a translation of the three poems see Iolo Goch, *Poems*, edited by Dafydd Johnston (Llandysul, 1993), pp.30-41.

[29] Gruffydd Aled Williams, 'Adolygu'r Canon: Cywydd arall gan Iolo Goch i Owain Glyndwr', *Llên Cymru*, XXIII (2000), 39-73.

[30] *Gwaith Gruffudd Llwyd a'r Llygliwiaid Eraill*, edited by Rhiannon Ifans (Aberystwyth, 2000), p.157.

[31] *Gwaith Gruffudd Llwyd*, pp.113-21.

[32] Iolo Goch, in the poem written at the height of Owain's rebellion, also compares Glyndŵr with Owain ab Urien, and adds a reference to a third heroic Owain: Owain Llawgoch. See Williams, 'Adolygu'r Canon', pp.64, 68-9. For Owain Llawgoch see A.D. Carr, *Owen of Wales: The End of the House of Gwynedd* (Cardiff, 1991).

[33] Thomson, *Owein*, pp.9, 11-12.

[34] *Gwaith Gruffudd Llwyd*, p.135.

[35] *Gwaith Gruffydd Llwyd*, p.146.

[36] *Gwaith Gruffudd Llwyd*, p.147.

[37] Davies, *Revolt of Owain Glyndŵr*, p.102.

[38] Davies, *Revolt of Owain Glyndŵr*, p.194.

[39] Lloyd, *Owen Glendower*, pp.143-5.

[40] *Gwaith Guto'r Glyn*, collectd by John Llywelyn Williams and edited by Ifor Williams (Cardiff, 1961), p.15.

[41] *Gwaith Dafydd Bach ap Madog Wladaidd, 'Sypyn Cyfeiliog' a Llywelyn ab y Moel*, edited by R. Iestyn Daniel (Aberystwyth, 1998), p.91.

[42] *Gwaith . . . Llywelyn ab y Moel*, p.95.

[43] *Gwaith . . . Llywelyn ab y Moel,* p.97. E.A. Rees, *Welsh Outlaws and Bandits: Political Rebellion and Lawlessness in Wales 1400-1603* (Birmingham, 2001), pp.99-100, includes Y Graig Lwyd, Cefn Digoll (Long Mountain) and Gwern y gof in Ceri among the localities that were 'notorious as bandit strongholds' in the fifteenth century.

[44] *Gwaith . . . Llywelyn ab y Moel,* pp.100, 152. See also Rees, *Welsh Outlaws and Bandits,* p.119.

[45] *Gwaith Guto'r Glyn,* p.15.

[46] *Gwaith . . . Llywelyn ab y Moel,* p.114.

[47] *Gwaith Gruffudd Llwyd,* p.179.

[48] *Gwaith Gruffudd Llwyd,* p.179-80.

[49] *Gwaith Gruffudd Llwyd,* p.180.

[50] *Gwaith Gruffudd Llwyd,* p.180.

[51] *Gwaith Gruffudd Llwyd,* pp.180-1.

[52] Roger L. Brown, *The Parish Church of St Mary of the Salutation, Welshpool: A Guide and History* (Welshpool, 2000), pp.1-2.

[53] *Gwaith Gruffudd Llwyd,* p.192.

[54] *Gwaith Gruffudd Llwyd,* pp.192-3.

[55] *Gwaith Gruffudd Llwyd,* p.193.

[56] *Gwaith Gruffudd Llwyd,* pp.193-4.

[57] *Gwaith Gruffudd Llwyd,* p.194.

[58] Thomas, *History,* III, 177; *Gwaith Gruffudd Llwyd,* p.309.

CONCLUSION

Cefn Digoll – the Long Mountain – was to be the scene of one more dramatic historic event. The failure of Owain Glyndŵr's rebellion had driven those poets who specialised in obscure prophetic pronouncements with a strong political slant to look for a new hero to save the Welsh people. As the Wars of the Roses created shifting alliances that produced rival claimants for the throne, there were several possible candidates to be the 'Mab Darogan' or 'Son of Prophecy'. Dafydd Llwyd ap Llywelyn ap Gruffydd of Mathafarn in the parish of Llanwrin in the far west of Powys Wenwynwyn was probably the greatest of the prophetic poets. His grandfather, Gruffudd ab Ieuan Llwyd, had been the subject of a praise poem composed by Gruffudd Llwyd, the poet of Glyndŵr and the Trinity.[1]

As a staunch Lancastrian supporter, Dafydd Llwyd of Mathafarn ended up identifying Henry Tudor (Harri Tudur) as the 'Mab Darogan'. There is even a tradition that the king-to-be spent the night at Mathafarn as he travelled towards Bosworth Field in 1485. It was at Cefn Digoll, on his way to that decisive battle, that Henry met up with the army of Sir Rhys ap Thomas, the most powerful figure in south and west Wales.[2] Sir Rhys's support would be one of the decisive factors in ensuring Henry's victory. Dafydd Llwyd was ecstatic in his praise of the new king (a prophetic poet who backs a winner must inevitably feel rather pleased with himself). He gloated that the 'mole' (Richard III) and his grandchildren had been killed:

> King Harri is conquering
> A golden crown, and he loves us.
> So the poets are happier:
> Winning the world and killing little R.,
> A grey, unhappy, forked letter,
> Not respected in England.[3]

And he sang:

Harri was, Harri shall be,
Harri is, long life to him![4]

Henry's success would be a mixed blessing even for those who regarded him as the ultimate hero. It led to the growing Anglicisation of the Welsh gentry and nobility and eventually to the Act of Union under the next Henry.

In the same year that the armies met in the shadow of the Long Mountain, the nearby abbey of Ystrad Marchell had a new abbot. D.R. Thomas records that Dafydd ab Owain 'was of the Glasgoed, Meifod, branch of the House of Dolobran'.[5] The abbot had studied law at Oxford, gaining the degree of D.C.L., and in the 1460s gave legal advice to the Yorkist earl of Gloucester, who was justice of North Wales. Then he switched sides to the Lancastrians, which stood him in good stead after Bosworth Field. He spent at least five and possibly ten years as abbot of Ystrad Marchell. From about 1495 to 1500 he was abbot of Ystrad Fflur (Strata Florida in Ceredigion) and then moved north to be abbot of Aberconwy from 1501-13, combining the post with that of bishop of St Asaph from 1504-13.[6]

Dafydd ab Owain was an extremely energetic man and a great restorer of buildings throughout his career, and no doubt he did any repairs that were necessary at Ystrad Marchell. However his most notable claim to fame was as an entertainer of poets. At least eleven poets are known to have sung Dafydd ab Owain's praises during his career, including some of the most distinguished bards of the period.[7] Those who addressed poems to him during his time at Ystrad Marchell included Tudur Aled, Dafydd ap Maredudd ap Tudur, Gruffudd ap Llywelyn Fychan, Bedo Brwynllys and Guto'r Glyn.[8] For a few years towards the end of the fifteenth century the Cistercian abbey in the Severn valley was a focus of Welsh poetic culture. Tudur Aled describes in graphic detail the feasts and the bounteous generosity that attracted the poets to Dafydd's monastery:

> What better lord is there for easy gifts, – the main course
> Venison or wild fowl?
> Who else has cooks preparing the ocean's fish,
> Just like a feast of Prester John's.
>
> Dishes of every kind, honeycombs from bees,
> German wines;

He brings us wine from Cheapside and the Isle of Opia,
And Genoa and good Alsatian osey

He gets the osey he wants from the cities,
And gives eighteen marks for Denmark wine;
Two shillings, forty shillings, ten shillings every day,
Ten thousand pounds, ten dishes daily,
There'll be ten hundred in his possession – always
Two more than an abbot who's a miser.[9]

With publicity like that it is hardly surprising that greedy, hungry and penniless poets flocked to Dafydd's abbey. It seems to have made Cefn Digoll, the nearby Long Mountain, synonymous with monastic generosity to poets, because Lewys Môn would write to Siôn Llwyd, abbot of Glyn-y-Groes (Valle Crucis), a few years later:

If the stones of Cefn Digoll
And the gravel and all the pebbles were gold,
You'd give them out of your generosity,
Abbot Siôn . . .[10]

The border bards were understandably depressed when abbot Dafydd moved on. Owain ap Llywelyn ab y Moel, son of the ex-outlaw poet buried in the abbey, remarked how respect for Ystrad Marchell had declined since Dafydd's departure.[11]

The poets were probably not the most reliable witnesses when it came to judging the achievements of abbots. It may be that the ultimate source of the financial problems and spiritual decay that the last abbot found when he came to Ystrad Marchell in 1527 was the startling extravagance of Dafydd ab Owain.[12] Which brings us back to where we began, with John ap Rhys, the Cistercian who liked to be known as 'Goyddvarche' or Gwyddfarch after the first abbot of Meifod, setting off sadly to London to surrender his monastery. It was 1536, the year of the Act of Union between England and Wales. After a thousand years the age of saints and heroes in the Powys borderland was finally at an end.

NOTES

[1] *Gwaith Gruffudd Llwyd,* pp.177-8.

[2] Enid Roberts, *Dafydd Llwyd o Fathafarn* (Caernarfon, 1981), p.31; Ralph A. Griffiths, *Sir Rhys ap Thomas and his Family: A Study in the Wars of the Roses and Early Tudor Politics* (Cardiff, 1993), p.42.

[3] *Gwaith Dafydd Llwyd o Fathafarn,* edited by W. Leslie Richards (Cardiff, 1964), p.69.

[4] *Gwaith Dafydd Llwyd o Fathafarn,* p.61.

[5] Thomas, *History,* I, 220-1.

[6] Thomas, *Charters,* p.50; Williams, *Welsh Cistercians,* I, 96-8.

[7] Williams, *Welsh Cistercians,* I, 97.

[8] Catrin T. Beynon Davies, 'Cerddi'r Tai Crefydd', M.A. thesis (University of Wales, Bangor, 1972), pp. 207-19.

[9] *Gwaith Tudur Aled,* edited by T. Gwynn Jones, 2 vols (Cardiff, 1926), I, 16.

[10] *Gwaith Lewys Môn,* p.239.

[11] *Gwaith Owain ap Llywelyn ab y Moel,* edited by Eurys Rolant (Cardiff, 1984), p.41.

[12] A single poem survives addressed to the last abbot of Ystrad Marchell. Huw Llwyd ap Dafydd ap Llywelyn ap Madog used his persuasive skills to request oxen from the hard-pressed cleric. The text is given in Davies, 'Cerddi'r Tai Crefydd', pp.220-1.

BIBLIOGRAPHY OF WORKS CITED

Andrews, Rhian M. and others (ed.), *Gwaith Bleddyn Fardd a Beirdd Eraill Ail Hanner y Drydedd Ganrif ar Ddeg* (Cardiff, 1996).

Ballinger, John and Fisher, John, *Y Llyfr Plygain 1612* (Cardiff, 1931).

Baring-Gould, S. and Fisher, John, *The Lives of the British Saints*, 4 vols (London, 1907-13).

Bartrum, Peter C., *A Welsh Classical Dictionary: People in History and Legend up to about A.D. 1000* (Aberystwyth, 1993).

Bede, *A History of the English Church and People* (Harmondsworth, 1965).

Bromwich, Rachel, Jarman, A.O.H. and Roberts, Brynley F. (ed.), *The Arthur of the Welsh: The Arthurian Legend in Medieval Welsh Literature* (Cardiff, 1991).

Bromwich, Rachel (ed.), *The Beginnings of Welsh Poetry: Studies by Sir Ifor Williams* (Cardiff, 1980).

Bromwich, Rachel (ed.), *Trioedd Ynys Prydein* (Cardiff, 1961).

Brown, Roger L., *The Parish Church of St Mary of the Salutation, Welshpool: A Guide and History* (Welshpool, 2000).

Burnham, Helen, *A Guide to Ancient and Historic Wales: Clwyd and Powys* (London, 1995).

Carr, A.D., *Owen of Wales: The End of the House of Gwynedd* (Cardiff, 1991).

Carr, A.D., 'Powys: Y Cefndir Hanesyddol yng Nghyfnod Beirdd y Tywysogion', *Llên Cymru* XXII (1999), 12-24.

Cartwright, Jane (ed.), *Celtic Hagiography and Saints' Cults* (Cardiff, 2003).

Cartwright, Jane, *Y Forwyn Fair, Santesau a Lleianod: Agweddau ar Wyryfdod a Diweirdeb yng Nghymru'r Oesoedd Canol* (Cardiff, 1999).

Chadwick, Nora, *The British Heroic Age: The Welsh and the Men of the North* (Cardiff, 1976).

Costigan, N.G., *Defining the Divinity: Medieval Perceptions in Welsh Court Poetry* (Aberystwyth, 2002).

Davies, Catrin T. Beynon, 'Cerddi'r Tai Crefydd', M.A. thesis (University of Wales, Bangor, 1972).

Daniel, R. Iestyn (ed.), *Gwaith Dafydd Bach ap Madog Wladaidd, 'Sypyn Cyfeiliog' a Llywelyn ab y Moel* (Aberystwyth, 1998).

Davies, John, *Hanes Cymru* (London, 1990).

Davies, Oliver and O'Loughlin, Thomas, *Celtic Spirituality* (New York and Mahwah, 1999).

Davies, R.R., *Lordship and Society in the March of Wales 1282-1400* (Oxford, 1978).

Davies, R.R., *The Age of Conquest: Wales 1063-1415* (Oxford, 1991).

Davies, R.R., *The Revolt of Owain Glyndŵr* (Oxford, 1995).

Davies, Wendy, *Wales in the Early Middle Ages* (Leicester, 1982).

Doble, Gilbert H., *The Saints of Cornwall, Part Five: Saints of Mid-Cornwall* (Oxford, 1970).

Dunlop, John B., *Staretz Amvrosy* (London, 1972).

Ellis, T.I., *Crwydro Maldwyn* (Llandybie, 1957).

Evans, D. Silvan (ed.), *Gwaith Y Parch. Walter Davies A.C. (Gwallter Mechain)*, 3 vols (Carmarthen, 1868).

Ford, Patrick K. (ed.), *Ystoria Taliesin* (Cardiff, 1992).

Fulton, Helen, 'Cyd-destun Gwleidyddol *Breudwyt Ronabwy*', *Llên Cymru* XXII (1999), 42-56.

Gerald of Wales, *The Journey Through Wales/The Description of Wales* (Harmondsworth, 1978).

Gould, Graham, *The Desert Fathers on Monastic Community* (Oxford, 1993).

Griffiths, Ralph A., *Sir Rhys ap Thomas and his Family: A Study in the Wars of the Roses and Early Tudor Politics* (Cardiff, 1993).

Gruffydd, R. Geraint (ed.), *Bardos: Penodau ar y Traddodiad Barddol Cymreig a Cheltaidd* (Cardiff, 1982).

Haycock, Marged, *Blodeugerdd Barddas o Ganu Crefyddol Cynnar* (Llandybie, 1994).

Haycock, Marged, 'Llyfr Taliesin: Astudiaethau ar rai agweddau', Ph.D. thesis (University of Wales, Aberystwyth, 1982).

Henken, Elissa, *The Welsh Saints; A Study in Patterned Lives* (Cambridge, 1991).

Henken, Elissa, *Traditions of the Welsh Saints* (Cambridge, 1987).

Henken, Elissa R., *National Redeemer: Owain Glyndŵr in Welsh Tradition* (Cardiff, 1996).

Higham, N.J., *The Kingdom of Northumbria AD 350-1100* (Stroud, 1993).

Ifans, Rhiannon (ed.), *Gwaith Gruffudd Llwyd a'r Llygliwiaid Eraill* (Aberystwyth, 2000).

Ifans, Rhiannon, *Gwerthfawrogi'r Chwedlau* (Aberystwyth, 1999).

Jackson, Kenneth (ed.), *Early Welsh Gnomic Poems* (Cardiff, 1973).

Jackson, Kenneth Hurlstone, *The Gododdin: The Oldest Scottish Poem* (Edinburgh, 1969).

Jarman, A.O.H., *Aneirin: Y Gododdin – Britain's Oldest Heroic Poem* (Llandysul, 1988).

Jarman, A.O.H. (ed.), *Llyfr Du Caerfyrddin* (Cardiff, 1982).

Johnston, Dafydd (ed.), *Galar y Beirdd: Marwnadau Plant/Poets' Grief: Welsh Elegies for Children* (Cardiff, 1993).

Johnston, Dafydd (ed.), *Gwaith Iolo Goch* (Cardiff, 1988).

Johnston, Dafydd (ed.), *Iolo Goch: Poems* (Llandysul, 1993).

Jones, Glyn and Morgan, T.J., *The Story of Heledd*, edited by Jenny Rowland (Newtown, 1994).

Jones, Morris Charles, 'The Abbey of Ystrad Marchell (Strata Marcella) or Pola', *Montgomeryshire Collections* IV (1871), 1-34, 293-322; V (1872), 109-48; VI (1873), 347-86.

Jones, Nerys Ann and Owen, Morfydd E., 'Twelfth-century Welsh hagiography: the *Gogynfeirdd* poems to saints' in Cartwright, Jane (ed.), *Celtic Hagiography and Saints' Cults* (Cardiff, 2003), pp.45-76.

Jones, Nerys Ann and Owen, Ann Parry (ed.), *Gwaith Cynddelw Brydydd Mawr*, 2 vols (Cardiff, 1991-5).

Jones, Rhys (ed.), *Gorchestion Beirdd Cymru neu Flodau Godidowgrwydd Awen* (Shrewsbury, 1773).

Jones, Thomas (trans.), *Brut y Tywysogyon or The Chronicle of the Princes: Peniarth MS 20 Version* (Cardiff, 1952).

Jones, T. Gwynn (ed.), *Gwaith Tudur Aled*, 2 vols (Cardiff, 1926).

Jones, Thomas Gwynn, *Y Dwymyn 1934-5* (Cardiff, 1972).

Lake, A. Cynfael (ed.), *Gwaith Siôn Ceri* (Aberystwyth, 1996).

Lloyd, J.E., *Owen Glendower* (Felinfach, 1992).

McGoldrick, James Edward, *Luther's English Connection* (Milwaukee, 1979).

McKenna, Catherine A., *The Medieval Welsh Religious Lyric: Poems of the Gogynfeirdd 1137-1282* (Belmont, Massachusetts, 1991).

Morgan, Enid (ed.), *Keep the Feast: An Introduction to Plygain* (Penarth, 2000).

Morris John (ed.), *Nennius: British History and The Welsh Annals* (London, 1980).

Owen, Morfydd E. and Roberts, Brynley F. (ed.), *Beirdd a Thywysogion: Barddoniaeth Llys yng Nghymru, Iwerddon a'r Alban* (Cardiff, 1996).

Pryce, H., 'A New Edition of the *Historia Divae Monacella*', *Montgomeryshire Collections*, LXXXII (1994), 23-40.

Pryce, Huw, *Native Law and the Church in Medieval Wales* (Oxford, 1993).

Rees, E.A., *Welsh Outlaws and Bandits: Political Rebellion and Lawlessness in Wales 1400-1603* (Birmingham, 2001).

Rhys, John (ed.), *Pennant's Tours in Wales*, 3vols (Caernarfon, 1883).

Rhys, John (ed.), *The Elucidarium and other tracts in Welsh from Llyvr Agkyr Llandewivrevi* (Oxfor, 1894).

Richards, Melville (ed.), *Breudwyt Ronabwy* (Cardiff, 1948).

Richards, W. Leslie (ed.), *Gwaith Dafydd Llwyd o Fathafarn* (Cardiff, 1964).

Roberts, Enid, *Braslun o Hanes Llên Powys* (Denbigh, 1965).

Roberts, Enid, *Dafydd Llwyd o Fathafarn* (Caernarfon, 1981).

Roberts, Thomas and Williams, Ifor (ed.) *The Poetical Works of Dafydd Nanmor* (Cardiff, 1923).

Robinson, David (ed.), *The Cistercian Abbeys: Far from the Concourse of Men* (London, 1998).

Rolant, Eurys (ed.), *Gwaith Owain ap Llywelyn ab y Moel* (Cardiff, 1984).

Rowland, Jenny, *Early Welsh Saga Poetry; A Study and Edition of the Englynion* (Cambridge, 1990).

Rowlands, Eurys I. (ed.), *Gwaith Lewys Môn* (Cardiff, 1975).

Smith, J. Beverley, *Llywelyn ap Gruffydd, Tywysog Cymru* (Cardiff, 1986).

The Dictionary of Welsh Biography down to 1940 (London, 1959).

Thomas, D.R., *The History of the Diocese of St Asaph*, 3 vols (Oswestry, 1908-13).

Thomas, Graham C.G. (ed.), *The Charters of the Abbey of Ystrad Marchell* (Aberystwyth, 1997).

Thomas, Gwyn, *Yr Aelwyd Hon* (Llandybie, 1970).

Thomas, Gwyn, *Y Traddodiad Barddol* (Cardiff, 1976).

Thomas, Patrick, *Illtud and his World* (Llantwit Major, 2000).

Thomas, R.S., *Poetry for Supper* (London, 1967).

Thomson, R.L (ed.), *Owein or Chwedyl Iarlles y Ffynnawn* (Dublin, 1975).

Wade-Evans, A.W. (ed.), *Vitae Sanctorum Britanniae a Genealogiae* (Cardiff, 1944).

Ward, Benedicta, *The Sayings of the Desert Fathers: The Alphabetical Collection* (London, 1975).

White, Roger and Barker, Philip, *Wroxeter: Life and Death of a Roman City* (Stroud, 1998).

Williams, David H., *The Welsh Cistercians*, 2 vols (Caldey Island, Tenby, 1984).

Williams, Glanmor, *Owen Glendower* (Oxford, 1996).

Williams, Glanmor, *The Welsh Church from Conquest to Reformation* (Cardiff, 1976).

Williams, Gruffydd Aled, 'Adolygu'r Canon: Cywydd arall gan Iolo Goch i Owain Glyndŵr', *Llên Cymru*, XXIII (2000), 39-73.

Williams, Gruffydd Aled (ed.), *'Canu Owain Cyfeiliog'* in *Gwaith Llywelyn Fardd I ac eraill o Feirdd y Ddeuddegfed Ganrif* (Cardiff, 1994), pp.191-277.

Williams, Gruffydd Aled, 'Owain Cyfeiliog: Bardd-dywysog?' in Owen, Morfydd E. and Roberts, Brynley F. (ed.), *Beirdd a Thywysogion: Barddoniaeth Llys yng Nghymru, Iwerddon a'r Alban* (Cardiff, 1996).

Williams, Ifor (ed.), *Canu Aneirin* (Cardiff, 1970).

Williams, Ifor (ed.), *Canu Llywarch Hen* (Cardiff, 1970).

Williams, Ifor (ed.) *Canu Taliesin* (Cardiff, 1960).

Williams, Ifor, *Chwedl Taliesin* (Cardiff, 1957).

Williams, Ifor, *Lectures on Early Welsh Poetry* (Dublin, 1970).

Williams, Ifor (ed.), *Pedeir Keinc y Mabinogi* (Cardiff, 1964).

Williams, J.E. Caerwyn and Lynch, Peredur I. (ed.), *Gwaith Meilyr Brydydd a'i Ddisgynyddion* (Cardiff, 1994).

Williams, John Llywelyn and Williams, Ifor (ed.), *Gwaith Guto'r Glyn* (Cardiff, 1961).

Williams, Waldo, *Cerddi* (Newtown, 1992).

Yr Eglwys yng Nghymru: Gwasanaethau'r Bore a'r Hwyr (Cowbridge, 1969).

Yr Eglwys yng Nghymru: Trefn y Foreol a'r Hwyrol Weddi (Penarth, 1984).